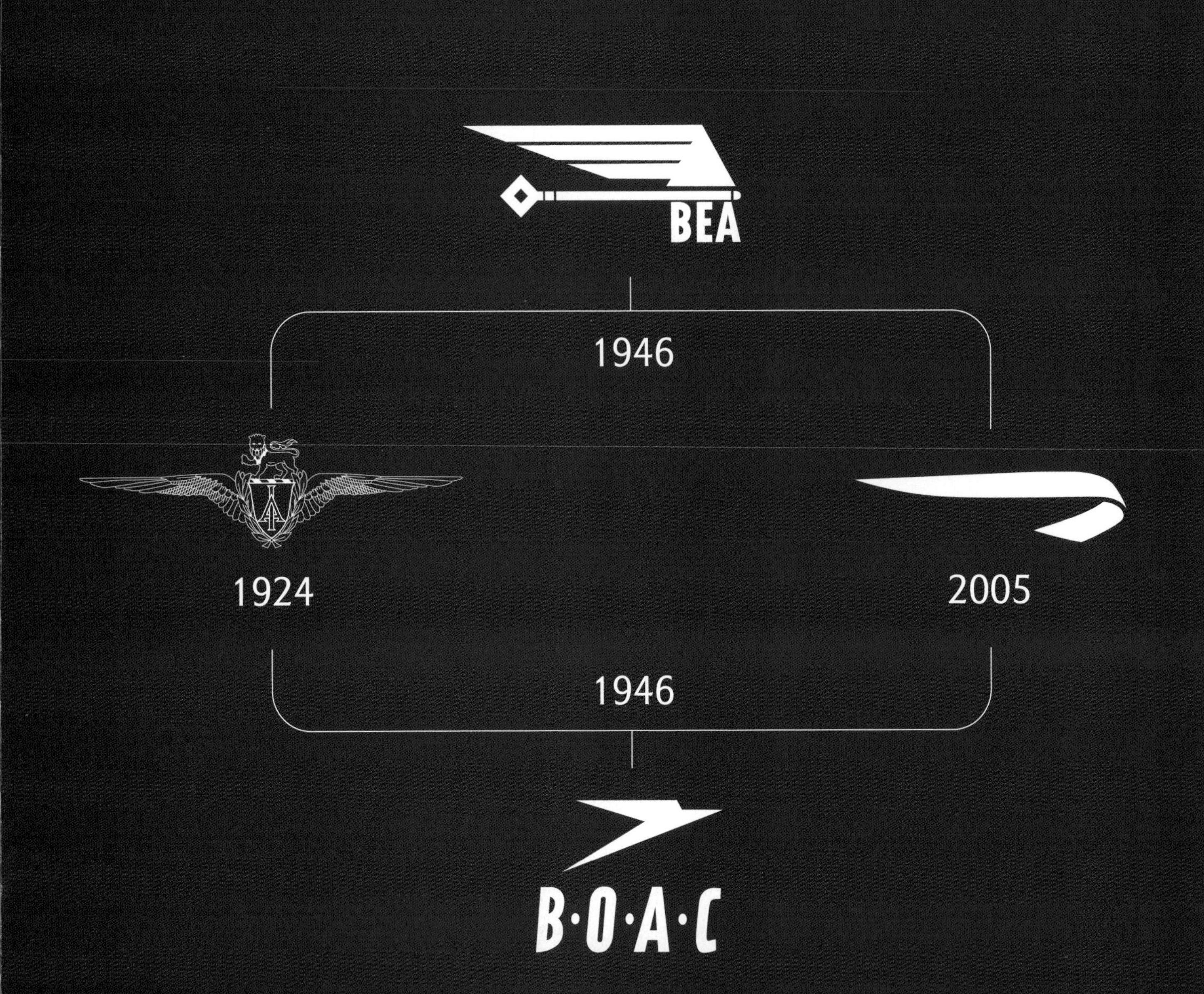
BEA
1946
1924
2005
1946
B·O·A·C

BUCKINGHAM PALACE

I warmly welcome all who are taking part in this commemoration of the Sixtieth Anniversary of the end of the Second World War.

Those of us who served in the War, whether in the Armed Forces or on the Home Front, and those who lost loved ones, will always remember that time with mixed feelings of pride and sadness.

I am sure that the programme of events today will provide many opportunities to reflect on that period of our history, and bring to the attention of today's generation the sacrifices which were made to ensure their freedom.

Elizabeth R

10th July, 2005.

By Tony Blair, Prime Minister

No-one living today can doubt the value of freedom and democracy. World War II was fought and won to secure the survival of those two principles.

The British people, together with those of the Commonwealth, the United States, France, Russia and other allies, committed themselves to that fight and, after long years of hardship, prevailed.

Had those who served this country failed, the result would have been invasion and occupation by a foreign power. Parliamentary government, which was born here, would have been suppressed. There would have been no freedom of speech or respect for human rights. The world would have been very different from the one we know today.

Since 1945 the world has changed immeasurably and there has been progress on a scale that would have been unimaginable at the end of the war. This would not have been possible without the lasting peace in Western Europe, gained for us by those who made their contribution to the war effort over those six years of struggle.

The world would have been very different from the one we know today

This is a time to remember and to give thanks to all of them. Huge numbers served in the armed forces and an equally essential contribution was made by those who worked on the home front, often in difficult or dangerous conditions. It was an unprecedented combined effort that achieved the victory.

It is right that on an occasion such as this, special tribute should be paid to those who gave their lives during the war. Most of us will also have proud memories of relations or friends who served in the war and have since died. But I am delighted that there are many other veterans of both the armed forces and the home front who are with us today. I should like to give them our heartfelt thanks. They have earned our utmost respect, gratitude and affection. ■

By the Chief of the Defence Staff, General **Sir Michael Walker** GCB, CMG, CBE, ADC Gen

Sixty years after the declaration of peace, we remember all those caught up in the largest and bloodiest war in history. In the Armed Forces, perhaps we think particularly of our predecessors who fought and made the ultimate sacrifice. But we think also of those who contributed in a wider sense.

Those who fought in the war are a dwindling number. Yet, every British family knows of relatives who are, or were, in one way or other, veterans of the conflict. Typically we think of 'veterans' as those deployed to North Africa, Italy, France or Malaya, to actively engage with the enemy. We are less likely to think of veterans as those who worked on the home front, civilian and military, in factories and fields, in support of the Forces abroad, or of the families broken up when loved ones were deployed overseas. We think of the 400,000 British people who died, but what of their bereaved families? These commemorations embrace the sacrifices made by people of all ages across all areas of society.

This year is also the 60th anniversary of the United Nations charter, signed in San Francisco by 50 nations, and providing us with the greatest worldwide mechanism that we have against threats to humanity. It was a charter strong enough to survive the subsequent Cold War, so that countries that lay on opposing sides of the Iron Curtain today deploy together on UN operations.

War also created a fierce collective determination within the Western world to ensure lasting peace and prosperity. The creation of NATO, and then the European Communities and the European free-trade area, which were to become the European Union, provided the necessary economic, diplomatic and military bonds to achieve that.

Today we face a very different enemy in the shape of terrorism. It is harder to predict because it represents no specific regime and originates from no specific geographical region. In working against it, those close international relations have become more important than ever. Few would have wished for war in 1939, but everyone today should recognise our debt to all those who worked, fought and made personal sacrifices to achieve the international strength and stability of the 21st century. ■

Jacob's then...

Think Jacob's and you'll no doubt immediately think of the famous cream cracker. Founded in 1839, Jacob's started as a small bakery in Waterford, baking bread, ship biscuits and selling barm for bread baking. They started making biscuits in Dublin in 1852.

The launch of the cream cracker

In 1880 a new type of biscuit arrived in Ireland. It was plain but crisp and more suited as a base for savoury food. The new biscuits had been invented in America and were called 'crackers'. George N. Jacob was dispatched to America to find out more about them. He arrived home armed with the know-how to produce a cracker that would, ultimately, leave all its rivals behind.

Experiments were carried out, and a cracker called 'Wave Crest' was launched; this survived until the 1930's. However in 1885 a new recipe and process was tested and Jacob's Cream Crackers were launched. The new cracker, a Jacob's original, was an instant success and quickly became the company's bestseller. By the early 1900's employment was above 1,300 and a second factory was opened in Aintree, Liverpool in 1912.

World War II.

As a result of the war, the factory switched production to Army biscuits, although there was still restricted production for civilian home consumption. Both the Dublin and Aintree factories produced 'ration' biscuits for the army and hundreds of tons were despatched to those in active service. Actual damage suffered at the Aintree factory was luckily confined to broken windows, but depots in Southampton and Birmingham were almost totally destroyed by enemy action. During the war Jacob's donated lorries to the Red Cross.

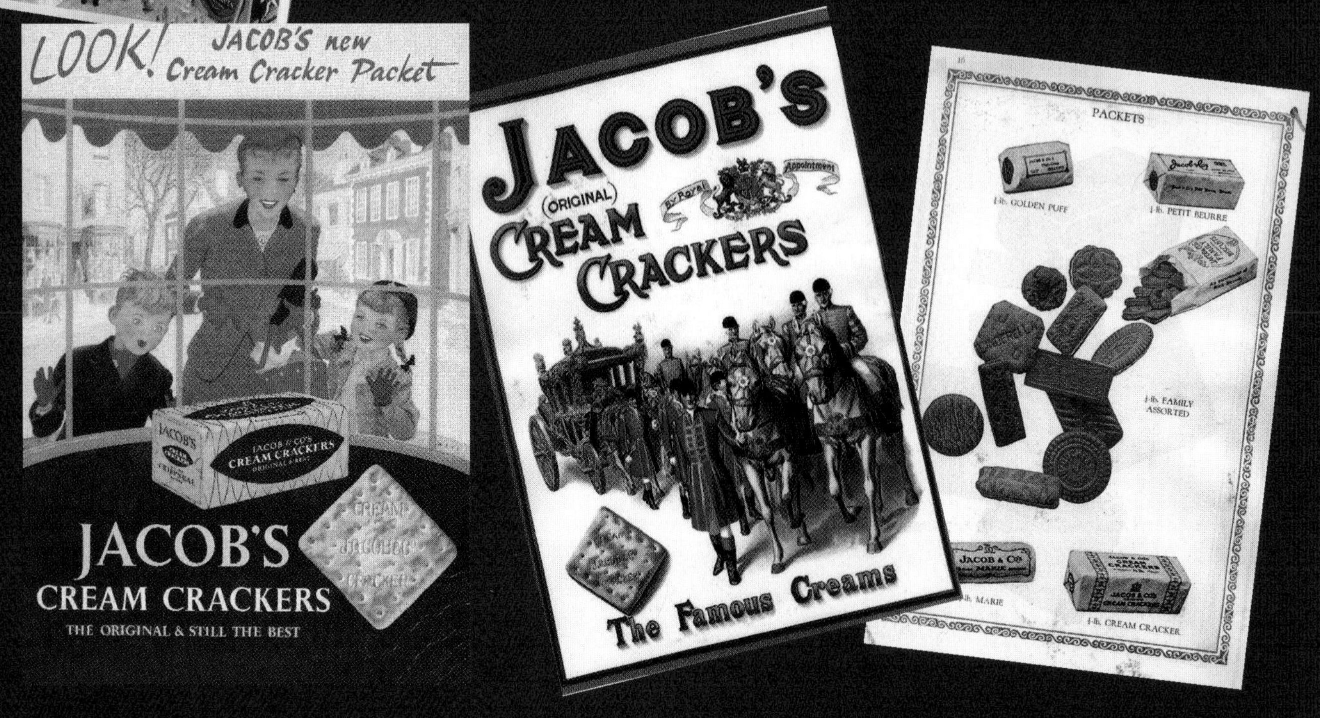

Thanks for our future

Editor	Alan Spence
Editorial Director	Claire Manuel
Managing Editor	Louise Drew
Editorial Co-ordinator	Zac Casey
Sub-editor	Nick Gordon
Art Editor	David Cooper
Designer	Emma McCaugherty
Production Director	Tim Richards
Sales Director	Andrew Howard
Sales Manager	John Storrie
Sales Executives	Andrew Adam Martin Murphy Rajeev Kapur
Client Services	Natalie Spencer
Publishing Services	David Ortiz
Development Director	Rebecca Henderson
Chief Operating Officer	Richard Linn
Chief Executive and Publisher	Alan Spence

Repro: ITM Publishing Services
Printed by William Gibbons
ISBN 1-901641-92-9

Published by
Newsdesk Communications Ltd,
130 City Road,
London EC1V 2NW, UK
Tel: +44 (0) 20 7650 1600
Fax: +44 (0) 20 7650 1609
www.newsdeskcomms.com

On behalf of the Ministry of Defence, MoD Main Building, Floor 8 Zone N, Whitehall, London SW1A 2HB
Tel: +44 (0) 20 7807 0978
Fax: +44 (0) 20 7218 5187

MINISTRY OF DEFENCE

Newsdesk Communications publishes a wide range of business and customer publications. For further information please contact Rebecca Henderson, Development Director.

Newsdesk Communications Ltd is a member of the Newsdesk Media Group of companies.

Photographs supplied by the Imperial War Museum. The Imperial War Museum has an incomparable collection covering all aspects of 20th and 21st century conflict involving Britain and the Commonwealth. The Museum's collections currently comprise over 19,000 works of art and 15,000 posters, objects ranging from aircraft to toy bears, 120 million feet of cine film, over 6 million photographs and 36,000 hours of oral history recordings, a huge range of documents, maps, diaries and letters, and a national reference library of over 270,000 items. For further information and online access to large parts of this rich resource visit www.iwmcollections.org.uk

Other photographs: Getty; Corbis; Camera Press London; British Antarctic Survey; David Secombe, Camera Press; britainonview; The National Archives; Plane Sailing; Royal British Legion.

The publishers would like to acknowledge the greatly valued support of Shell in contributing towards the success of this commemorative project

Contents

Message from the Queen

5 Her Majesty the Queen

Forewords

7 Prime Minister Tony Blair

9 Chief of the Defence Staff, General Sir Michael Walker GCB, CMG, CBE, ADC Gen

Introduction

25 Alan Spence, Editor, *Thanks for our future*

The campaigns

29 The man who gave the roar
Alan Spence

30 Battle on the seas
The battle for naval supremacy
Paul Beaver

34 Battle on the ground
Outlining the major land campaigns
Stephen Bungay

40 Battle in the skies
The instrumental role of the RAF in the Allied victory
Paul Beaver

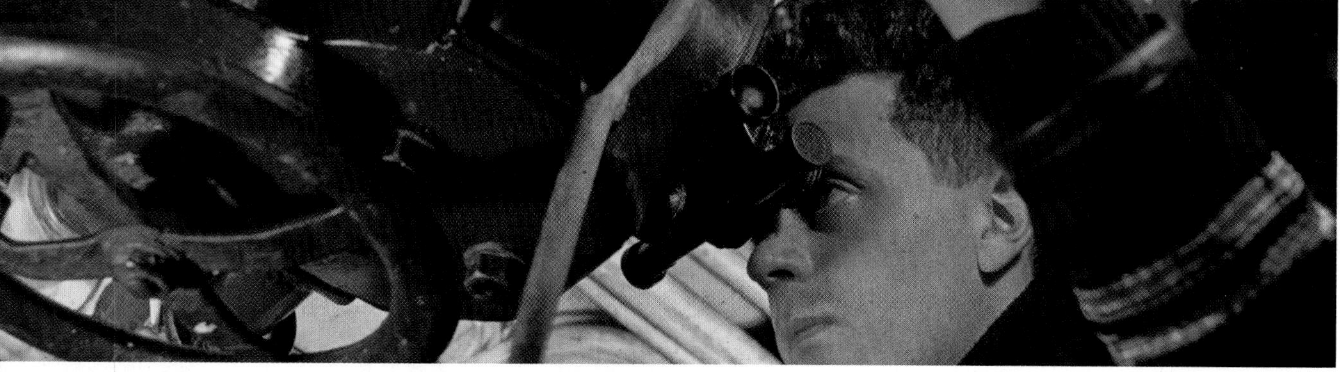

INTERCONTINENTAL.
HOTELS GROUP

INTERCONTINENTAL.
HOTELS & RESORTS

CROWNE PLAZA
HOTELS & RESORTS

Holiday Inn
HOTELS · RESORTS

Express
by Holiday Inn

STAYBRIDGE
SUITES

People at war

47 Unsung heroes
The heroism of ordinary people in everyday life
Richard Morris

50 Blood ties
The effects of wartime disruption to family life
Maureen Waller

58 Women's work
Recognising the crucial role that women played during the conflict
Peri Hope Langdale

66 Through the eyes of a child
Recollections of life as a child during the war
David Childs

70 Vital connections
Wartime postal services and their contribution to the war effort
Richard Morris

74 Food for thought
How rationing transformed eating habits
Carol Wilson

80 Safety first
Safety precautions and their effect on the British public
David Childs

85 Learning the hard way
The war led to disruption to schooling and changes in education
David Childs

Special events

92 St James's Park
Veterans Awareness Week

93 The Living Museum
A taste of wartime life

94 Veterans' Centre
A place to meet and relax

95 Military vehicles
Vehicles that saw action during the war

96 'Warriors for the Working Day'
An exhibition of wartime art

98 Sounding a warning
How church bells helped keep Britain alert
Prebendary John Scott

99 Images from the archive
Giant images from World War II projected onto Buckingham Palace
Sheelagh Barnard

101 Vintage aircraft flypast
A guide to the World War II planes taking part

Lifestyle

110 Make-do and mend
The creativity and resourcefulness of wartime fashion
Lauren Rose-Smith

115 Playing the game
Sport takes a back seat
Roger Linn

121 A night at the pictures
Escapism and propaganda at the cinema
Robin Cross

126 Tuned in
Informing and entertaining the public
Howard Gossington

131 Raising a glass to the future
The pub as a mainstay of the community
Roger Linn

135 Keeping up morale
The role of the media in the war
Howard Gossington

Contents

Work and travel

141 The industrial effort
Harnessing national resources
Paul Beaver

146 Business as usual
Supporting and providing for the war effort
Andrew Maiden

153 The power of invention
Advances and innovation in technology
Paul Beaver

158 Staying on track
The resilience of the railways
Christian Wolmar

In defence of the realm

166 Defending our people
The importance of civil defence
Roger J.C. Thomas

172 Defending our shores
The construction of coastal ground defences
William Foot

178 Defending our skies
Ground crews' essential role in air defence
Richard Morris

Caring and remembrance

186 Continuing support
The work of the Royal British Legion
Andrew Maiden

188 A vital network
The role of the British Red Cross
Zac Casey

190 In memoriam
Remembering the sacrifice of so many
Paul Beaver

194 Acknowledgements

196 War is over!
The nation celebrates
Louise Drew

198 Advertiser index

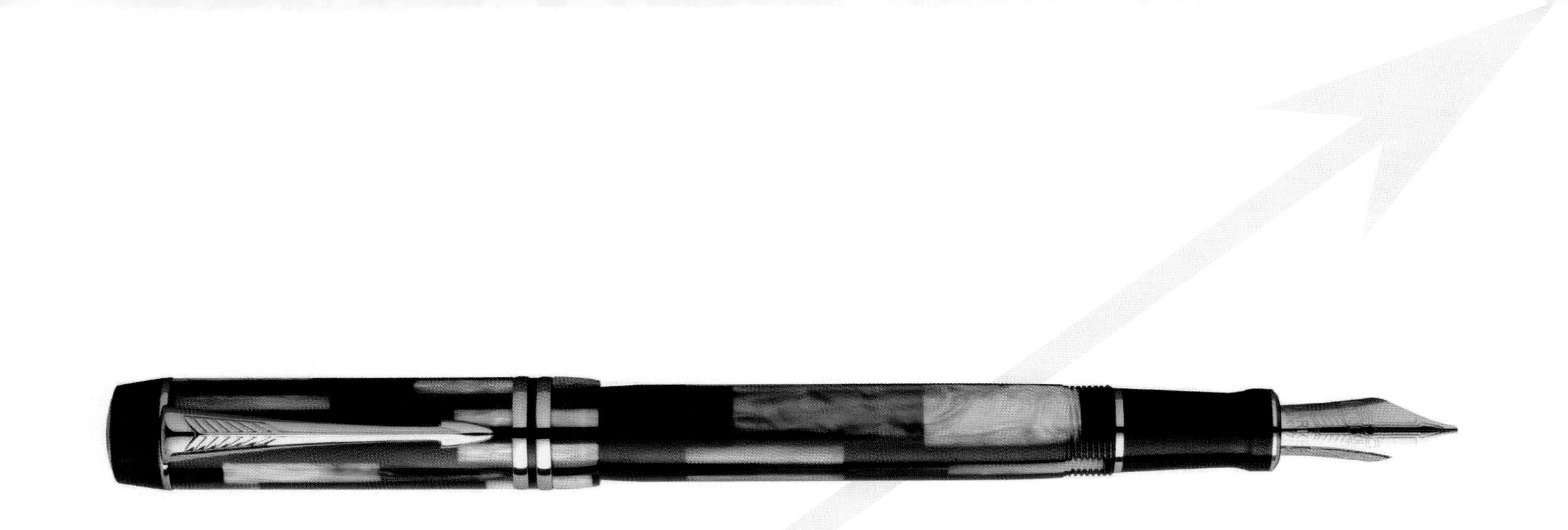
The King of Pens. And vice-versa.
The Parker Duofold.
PARKER®

BY APPOINTMENT TO H.M. THE QUEEN
MANUFACTURERS OF PENS, PENCILS AND INKS
PARKER PEN COMPANY, NEWHAVEN, ENGLAND
BY APPOINTMENT TO H.R.H. THE PRINCE OF WALES
MANUFACTURERS OF WRITING INSTRUMENTS AND INKS
PARKER PEN COMPANY, NEWHAVEN, ENGLAND

RKS & SPENCER
RKS &
ENCER
LTD
OPEN HERE
OPENING

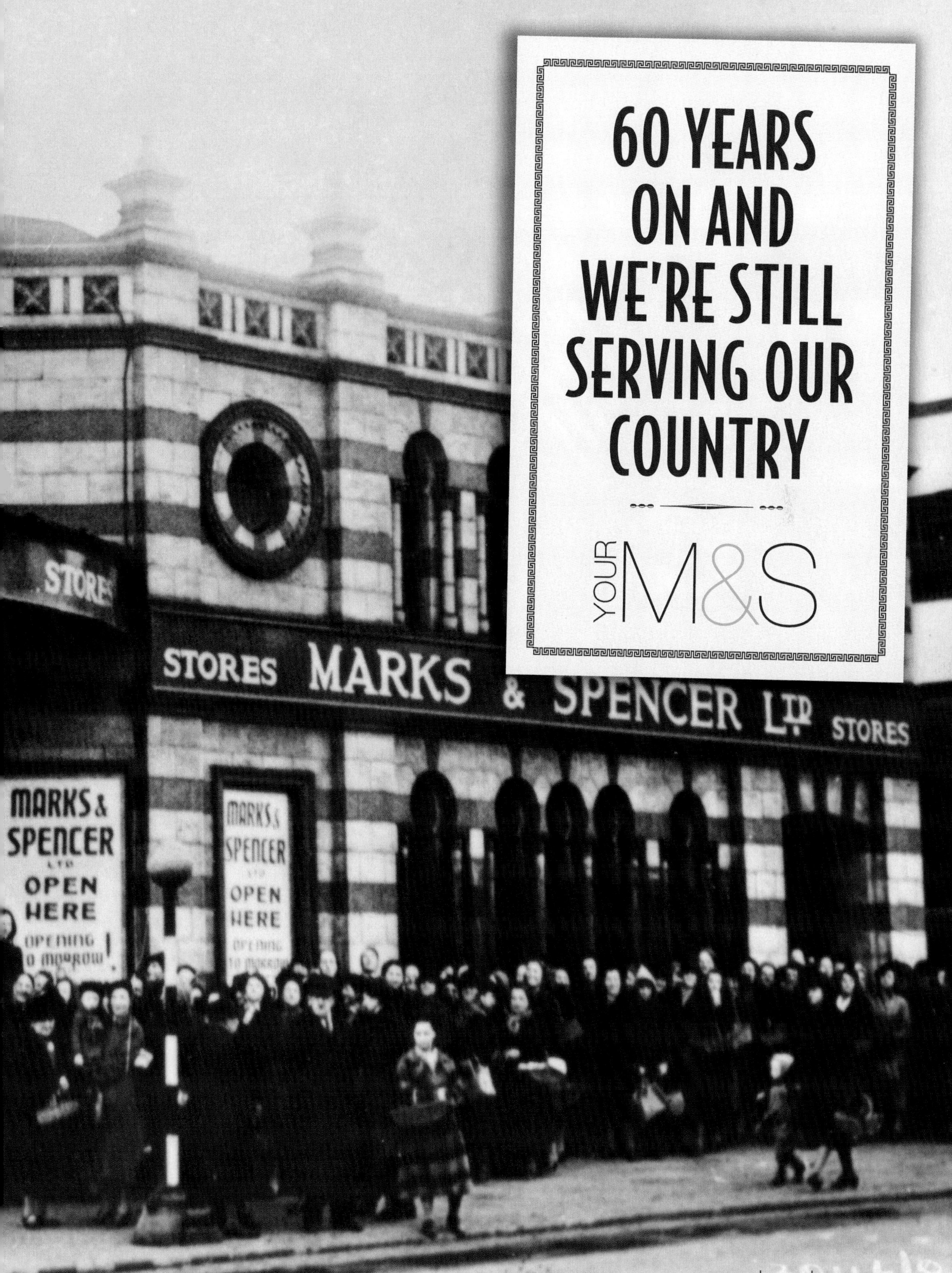
60 YEARS ON AND WE'RE STILL SERVING OUR COUNTRY
YOUR M&S
STORES MARKS & SPENCER LTD STORES
MARKS & SPENCER LTD OPEN HERE OPENING TOMORROW
MARKS & SPENCER LTD OPEN HERE OPENING TOMORROW

By **Alan Spence, Editor,**
Thanks for our future

World War II was the People's War. Never before had British life, British society been so overwhelmingly mobilised for what became total war – from fire hearths, playing fields and factories to sea, land and air battles in some of the remotest parts of the world.

For those generations caught up in the People's War, hardship, suffering, sacrifice and death became for nearly six years a way of life. In his immortal words, all Britain's Prime Minister Winston Churchill said he could offer the British people was "blood, toil, tears and sweat". And that was precisely what they got.

For those generations caught up in the People's War, hardship, suffering, sacrifice and death became a way of life

This publication is about those generations of 60 years ago who, during World War II, grew up, grew old, fought at home or overseas, farmed the land, worked in the factories by day and night, guarded their homeland and eventually fought Britain's enemies back to theirs. It is about the physical and emotional deprivations they suffered. About – whether at home or overseas – how they lived and loved and often died.

In describing their lives and what often ordinary people achieved from the kitchen front to the battle front, this publication serves as a tribute to their fortitude and bravery, and acts as a commemoration of their great collective achievements, which ultimately led to victory.

It is also a reminder for today's generations, who had no direct involvement in the conflict, of the great debt of gratitude they owe those who sacrificed so much to free Britain from the threat of foreign tyranny and preserve British freedom for the generations to come.

This publication also stands as an historical record of the dramatic, traumatic events that engulfed Britain from 1939 to 1945. These pages will hopefully convey to the reader what it was like to be there – how people clothed themselves, adjusted to food rations, were entertained; how children were evacuated, women worked in the factories and on the land; how people stayed as safe as they could in crowded air-raid shelters night after night and how, finally, they spilled in to the streets in joyous celebration on VE and VJ Day in 1945.

Many have contributed their memories or recalled the memories of others – and we thank them all. It is perhaps time now for younger generations to increasingly carry these memories forward to help ensure that they never die. ■

The mechanical hero was the Supermarine Spitfire

The Royal Navy built up a major amphibious force

The campaigns

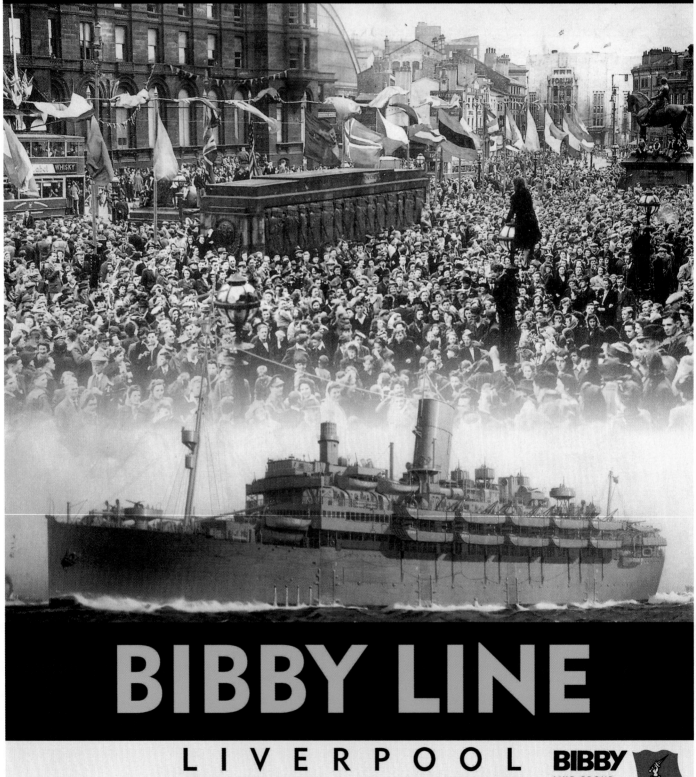

The man who gave the roar

Winston Churchill personified Britain's wartime spirit, courage and resilience. By **Alan Spence**

"It was a nation and race dwelling all round the globe that had the lion heart. I had the luck to be called upon to give the roar". So said Sir Winston Churchill, Britain's indomitable wartime leader from the dark days of 1940, when the country stood alone against Nazi Germany, to the relief and joy of victory in May 1945.

On the day war ended with Germany, May 8, Churchill addressed massed crowds from a balcony in Whitehall. "This is your victory," he told them, the nation and the world. "It is the victory of the cause of freedom in every land. In all our long history we have never seen a greater day than this."

After the defeat of the British Expeditionary Force in 1940 and its evacuation from Dunkirk, invasion by Germany was a very real possibility. But like so many of the people he led, Churchill never countenanced the idea of defeat or some form of peace deal with the Nazis. "We shall never surrender," he declared.

Years later, when making him an honorary citizen of the United States, President John F. Kennedy spoke of how, in Britain's darkest hour, Churchill's brilliant oratory had "mobilised the English language and sent it into battle".

In 1940, defiance may not have been logical, but it proved to be the right strategy and laid the foundation stones of eventual victory. Churchill personified it.

"You ask what is our policy? I can say: it is to wage war by sea, land and air, with all our might and with all the strength that God can give us; to wage war against a monstrous tyranny, never surpassed in the dark, lamentable catalogue of human crime.

"You ask what is our aim? I can answer in one word: it is victory, victory at all costs, victory in spite of all terror, victory however long and hard the road may be; for without victory, there is no survival."

The road was indeed long and hard. Many died and many suffered terrible injuries, couples and families were parted – some of them forever.

Churchill's personality combined so many of the characteristics of the British war effort, both at home and overseas. Defiance and daring, cussed resistance, burning hope and an unshakeable belief, initially against all odds, that Britain would survive, ultimately triumph and that Britons' freedom would be secured for future generations. ■

The role of the British Navy was crucial throughout the conflict. **Paul Beaver** describes how its brave men and women played their part

Battle on the seas

Britain is now and has been a maritime trading-nation for a millennium. If the beginning of World War II (WWII) was 'phoney' to those in the British Army and Royal Air Force in Europe, Africa and Asia, it was not for the Royal Navy. Merchant ships and the fishing fleet had to be protected, convoys organised, mines hunted and destroyed and the German submarine fleet – the dreaded U-Boats – engaged on a daily basis.

Success came early to the Royal Navy's South Atlantic Fleet. Trapping the German high-seas raider, *Admiral Graf Spee*, in a South American estuary, the cruiser force of Commodore (later Admiral) Harwood scored the first victory of a six-year war. The prisoners taken during *Admiral Graf Spee*'s commerce-raiding in the Indian Ocean and South Atlantic were held aboard the German merchant ship, *Altmark*.

Altmark tried to sail back to Germany via neutral Norway's coastal waters. The Royal Navy, however, was having none of that and sent Captain (later Admiral) Vian in the destroyer HMS *Cossack* to intercept it and release the prisoners. *Cossack*'s company did this with the cry, "The Navy's here lads!"

Norway was again centre stage for a naval engagement a year later. In May 1941, the major units of the Royal Navy were mobilised against the threat of the brand new and powerful German 'pocket' battleship, *Bismarck*, which moved into the North Atlantic to engage convoys. That she did not do, being sent to the bottom by Force H from Gibraltar, but not before sinking the pride of the British fleet, 'Mighty' HMS *Hood*.

Convoys in the Atlantic bridge between North America and the United Kingdom were to be

The Royal Navy built up a major amphibious force

background to all naval operations from 1939 to VE Day in 1945. The Royal Navy and the Merchant Navy lost several thousand ships to the marauding submarines and bombers of the German war machine.

For a spell too, convoys were being run to Russia's northern ice-free ports, also running the gauntlet of bombers, submarines and the occasional major surface-warship. Despite the cost in lives and shipping, the convoys kept the Soviet war machine going during the bleak period immediately after Hitler's invasion in 1941.

Natural battlegrounds

In warmer waters, in the early war years, the Mediterranean Fleet, based in Alexandria and later Malta, ruled what the Italian fascist leader, Mussolini, once had the temerity to call the 'Italian Lake'. The Italian Fleet of modern battleships and cruisers outclassed the Royal Navy's monoliths from WW1, yet Admiral Cunningham's Nelson-style tactics at Cape Matapan, and his veteran Swordfish torpedo-bombers at Taranto, sank the Italian Fleet and cleared the 'Lake' for a year, until overwhelming German air and naval forces made an appearance.

It took nearly two more years to redress the balance, pushing the Germans to retreat and Italy to surrender. This period included the dreadful siege of Malta, during which the island was one of the most intensely bombed areas in the entire war, yet the population of 270,000 stood firm throughout. Acknowledging such bravery, on April 15 1942 King George VI made a unique award: he bestowed the George Cross to the Maltese nation, which to this day is still borne by the Maltese on their flag.

The narrow seas of the English Channel, North Sea, Adriatic and Aegean in the Mediterranean were the natural battlegrounds for the Coastal Forces. Mainly manned by officers and men of the Royal Naval Volunteer Reserve, the motor torpedo boats and motor-launches attacked enemy shipping, harassed shore bases and worked closely with partisan forces determined to liberate their countries from the Nazi yoke.

A move to the east

As the war progressed, and under the guidance of the Commander-in-Chief of Combined Operations, Admiral Lord Mountbatten, the Royal Navy built up a major amphibious force that cut its teeth at Dieppe in 1942. Thus, it was ready for the world's largest-ever naval task force, landing troops and equipment over the beaches of Normandy on D-Day (June 6 1944).

Just as Malta was being assaulted by the combined German and Italian air forces, the Japanese Naval Air Force engaged and sank two capital ships, including the new heavy cruiser, HMS *Prince of Wales*. She had been

"Aye, we had a great time"

Daniel Upex joined the Merchant Navy in the Boys' Services at the age of 15, and served from 1943 to 1947. His memories are happy ones. "I enjoyed the lot – the navy was great fun. The best time was getting drunk. Aye, we had a grand time."

He travelled all over the world, on 13 different ships. He only ran into trouble with enemy submarines once, when he took part in the Russian convoys. It was Christmas 1944, and they had travelled to Minsk in a convoy of 15 destroyers and two cruisers. As they were leaving the harbour, the Germans were waiting for them and an enemy submarine sunk one of their destroyers. Luckily for Daniel, he survived and, despite making many trips around the world, he didn't run into any more problems, aside from rough weather.

One thing he remembers clearly about the D-Day invasions was sleeping on board and suddenly being woken up by a massive bang. Their ship had shot down a German plane. He jumped up and ran on deck to see what was going on and realised that he had missed the action. "That was some wake-up call." When he came out of the services, Daniel went to work on the railroads and then the buses. "I wish I'd never come out though; the Merchant Navy was the most fun!"

present at the 'Hunt for the Bismarck' and her loss was a genuine blow to the pride of the Royal Navy.

It took three years for the Royal Navy to return and battle in earnest with the Imperial Japanese Navy. Technology had improved by then, as had the numbers and quality of the sailors. On the other hand, the Japanese were on the back foot and retreating from Burma, Siam (now Thailand) and, eventually, the Malayan Peninsula.

By mid-1944, with the German High Seas Fleet either sunk or stuck in port, the main surface action moved to the East. The British Pacific Fleet, with newly commissioned battleships and cruisers, based around a dozen aircraft carriers, which carried purpose-built fighters and torpedo-bombers, crewed by a new generation of sailors, was in action from late-1944.

These battle groups of larger carriers were in the thick of it, attacked by Japanese kamikazes (fighter-type aircraft packed with explosives, which were flown by dive-bombing suicide pilots) but ultimately seeing the Japanese surrender in Tokyo Bay in August 1945. The Light Fleet carriers undertook the liberation of Singapore and Hong Kong, racing against time to bring food and medical supplies to thousands of prisoners of war and interned civilians.

The Royal Navy ended WWII as the world's second-largest fleet, sailing the seven seas and arguably, with the Merchant Navy, having saved Britain from starvation in the dark period of 1941-42. Its men and women had been on every sea and ocean and were found 'not wanting'. ■

Dr Stephen Bungay outlines the major land campaigns that took place during the conflict

Battle on the ground

In the six years of World War II (WWII), the British Army fought in Europe, Africa and Asia. Its first actions came in the form of hasty, poorly organised attempts to challenge the German invasion of Norway in April 1940. Small bodies of troops were put ashore with little support and evacuated within a couple of weeks. The campaign led directly to the resignation of the Prime Minister Neville Chamberlain, and his replacement on the evening of May 10 with Winston Churchill.

That very morning, the German Wehrmacht had launched an assault on France and the Low Countries. As the British Expeditionary Force (BEF) advanced into Belgium, German armour surged unexpectedly out of the Ardennes forest and raced for the Channel coast. In danger of being cut off, the BEF retreated to Dunkirk, where most of its surviving men were evacuated, leaving their equipment behind. On June 22 1940, France surrendered.

Having failed to gain air superiority over south-east England and the English Channel, Hitler decided not to attempt invasion. He left Britain under siege from U-boats and sporadic air attacks, isolated but undefeated, while in June 1941 his military might turned on the Soviet Union. For the next two years, British and German troops only formally confronted each other in the deserts of North Africa.

Italy had declared war on Britain in June 1940, and in September invaded Egypt. A small mobile British force counter-attacked and by the end of the year had driven the Italians back into Libya. The following

Hitler decided not to attempt invasion

spring, the British captured Italy's colonies in East Africa. But by then, German forces under General (later Field Marshal) Rommel had arrived in the desert and begun a two-year campaign that see-sawed across North Africa until, in the summer of 1942, the two sides reached stalemate at the only part of the desert not passable to the south, known as the Alamein line.

Changing fortunes

The summer of 1942 marked the low point of the war for Britain. Since 1940, things had got steadily worse. In December 1941 the Japanese launched themselves at the British Empire in the East, culminating in February 1942 in the surrender of the garrison of Singapore, one of the greatest disasters in the history of the British Army. By the end of May, the Japanese had occupied Burma and threatened India. In the desert, the fortress town of Tobruk was taken by the Germans in June.

Yet at that point, the fortunes of war changed, and the change was permanent.

The war against the Germans changed in October 1942, when the British Eighth Army, under a new commander, General Montgomery, launched an assault

"We made the most of the time we had"

Marion Taylor served in the Army from 1941-1946 as a Bombardier in the 444 Ack Ack Battery (part of 125 Regiment).

Marion was based in the UK and she first worked on a predictor in the Ack Ack battery. When a plane was sighted, they gave the range and had to focus on getting the plane in line with the predictor. Using a telescope with a cross at the end of it, they lined it up with the plane. When all the dials were lined up properly and each girl was lined up properly, then that information from the dials (height, bearing etc) was sent to the guns, which then used these to fire at the planes.

Marion also worked on the searchlights. On one occasion when she was number one on the searchlight, Marion remembers a German plane coming right down the beam of the searchlight, machine-gunning right at her. When they spotted an enemy plane, they would send out the alarm, put out the light, and run for the slit trenches. On this particular occasion Marion remembers that when they jumped in the trench the air was filled with screaming; not because of the enemy, but because the trenches were filled with icy water.

Marion enjoyed her time in the Army. She put on a very brave face, although it was a frightening time, especially at the beginning. "We were frightened but tried not to show it." On her first night on active duty, Marion remembers, "I've never been so scared in my life. I'll always remember it; we were near South Shields and the German plane came down shooting right at us. Although I was really frightened, I was more scared of showing my fear. Apparently I did a good job, as my sergeant came over and asked me if I could read a range control card, as he said I didn't look frightened and the girl who was supposed to be doing it was petrified with fear. I managed to do it somehow, even though for a while I was holding it upside down!"

Marion made wonderful friends during the war. "These were friends like you'll never get again in your life. We made the most of the time we had and lived for every day, we just had to go with the flow."

German forces under General Rommel had arrived in the desert and begun a two-year campaign that see-sawed across North Africa

on the German-Italian positions at the Alamein line. It was a World War I-style slogging match, and it was decisive. The Eighth Army broke through and pursued their enemies into Tunisia, where it was joined by the First Army as the Germans also poured in reinforcements. Finally, in May 1943, the German-Italian Army in Africa surrendered, with losses that began to reach the scale of the Eastern front.

Two months later the Allies invaded Sicily, and after its fall the Eighth Army pursued the Germans up the toe of Italy, beginning a campaign in what Churchill called the "soft under-belly" of Europe. It turned out to be a hard and scaly backbone. After narrowly managing to secure a further beachhead at Salerno, the Allies began a long, slow series of river crossings, pushing the Germans back to fortified positions south of Rome that centred on the formidable mountains around Cassino. Assaults on this position were carried out in wretched conditions for the first six months of 1944 until, with a further beachhead established behind the position at Anzio, the Germans finally withdrew and Rome was liberated on June 4.

It was at this time that the war against the Japanese reached its turning point. In Burma, the 14th Army, under General William Slim, slowly learned how to deal with the jungle as well as their enemy and, in the spring of 1944, decisively defeated an attempted Japanese invasion of India at the twin battles of Imphal and Kohima. Exploiting command of the air to supply his troops, Slim took the offensive and began the reconquest of Burma.

Tightening the noose

All these events were overshadowed in the public mind by Operation Overlord, the invasion of Normandy, the largest seaborne operation in history, launched on D-

"The jungle was miserable"

Jim Lennon was an anti-aircraft gunner, serving in the army for the duration of the war. He manned 3.7in anti-aircraft guns. These were one of the largest kinds of gun, and they took them into the Burmese jungle because they had little manoeuvrability. His role in the jungle was to snipe at the Japanese from 12 miles away. Being an anti-aircraft gunner meant he was constantly on the go. "This was a good thing; there was no sitting about waiting for action. We joined up because we wanted action and we certainly got it!"

Jim is from Northern Ireland. All those who joined the regiment in Ireland were volunteers. Jim decided to join up because of the feeling of camaraderie. His entire regiment of 1,200 was made up of Belfast men and they were all friends – his entire street joined up. "We all knew each other; it was like one big family. Because of this it was fun at times, although other times were terrible. Thank God we all had each other!"

In 1942 Jim was sent to Burma, and he and his regiment were the first army to stay in the jungle during the monsoon – in fact they stayed in the Burmese jungle for three years. "The jungle was miserable," he recalls. "It was hot and sticky and wet. We had ringworm and every blooming thing; it was bloody awful! But all your own kind was with you, so it wasn't so bad."

Day, June 6 1944. In the weeks following D-Day, Allied ground-forces fought a bitter battle of grinding attrition, with the British and Canadians of 21st Army Group drawing the bulk of the German Panzer Divisions onto their front, until the German lines broke. By launching a counter-attack towards the west, Hitler pushed his forces into a noose, which closed at Falaise in August. Almost the whole of the German Army in the west was destroyed, Paris fell and the Allies drove eastwards in pursuit, until they outran their supply lines.

In September, seeking to sustain momentum, the Allies spread a carpet of paratroopers across the Netherlands to capture key bridges for ground forces to pass over and enter Germany. The final bridge at Arnhem proved to be a bridge too far and

The campaigns

the 1st Airborne Division had to be evacuated. This failed gamble condemned 21st Army Group to a miserable winter of slow, piecemeal gaining of ground in the face of determined opposition, clearing the Dutch coastal islands and securing enough space in the area west of the Rhine to launch a crossing of the river itself.

Allied operations were disrupted just before Christmas 1944 by the German Army's last offensive in the West, known as the Battle of the Bulge because of the salient it created in the American lines. With help from British forces, the Americans held and pushed back the Germans, and preparations for the crossing of the Rhine resumed. That finally came in March 1945 and led to the encirclement of German forces in the Ruhr, enabling 21st Army Group to occupy most of northern Germany by the time of the Nazi surrender in May 1945. By this time the 8th Army in Italy had reached the Po Valley and by the time Japan surrendered in August, 14th Army occupied the whole of Burma.

Every theatre of the ground war had horrors of its own, but the strains, privations and sufferings of the common solider were similar in kind. In the British Army, casualty rates among front-line soldiers were similar to those of World War I. It was common for two-thirds of an infantry battalion to become casualties in the course of a campaign. Those who came through WWII had endured the most destructive conflict in human history. ■

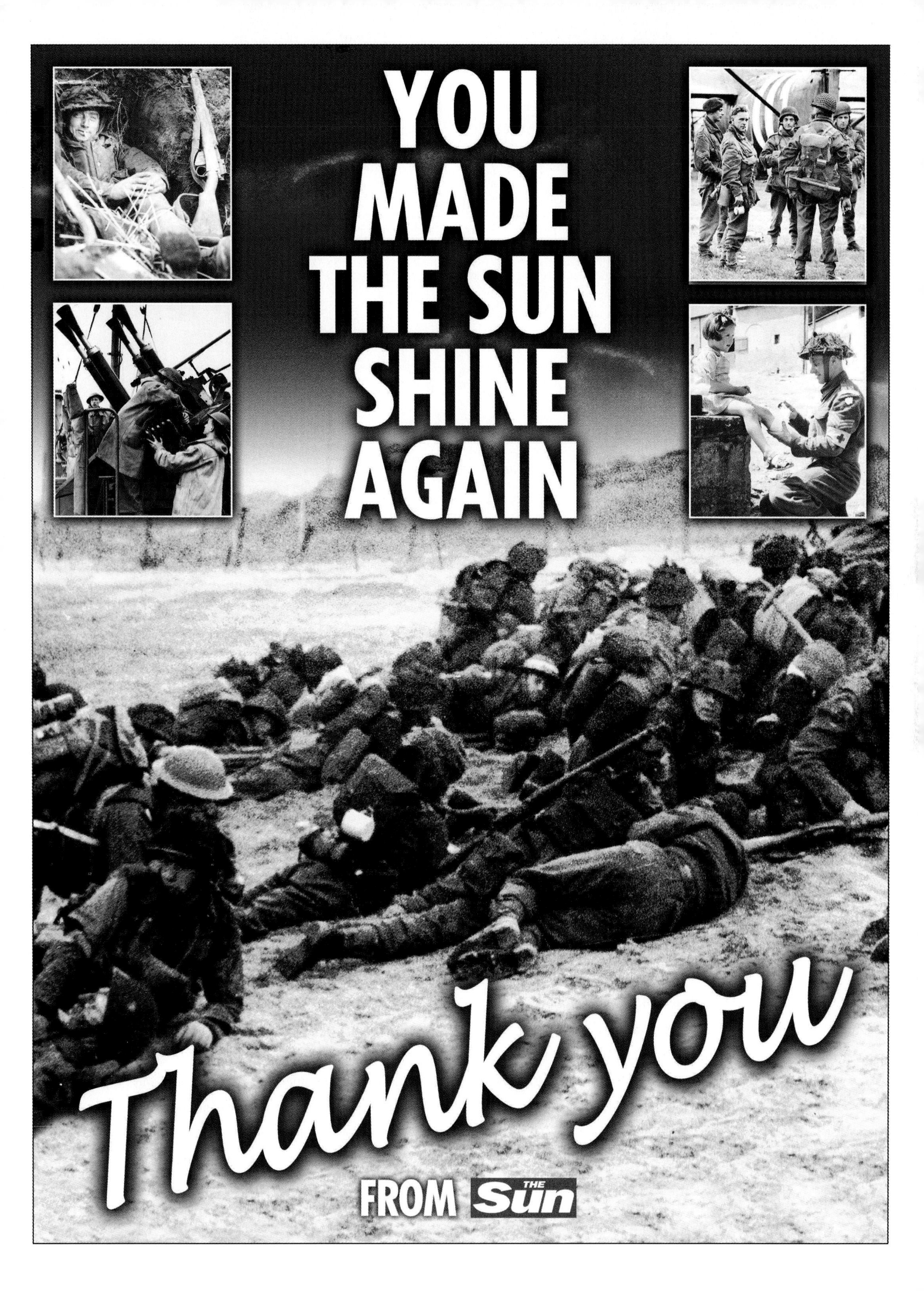
YOU
MADE
THE SUN
SHINE
AGAIN
Thank you
FROM THE Sun

Battle in the skies

The Royal Air Force played an instrumental part in the war effort. **Paul Beaver** takes a look back at the air campaigns that helped to ensure the Allied victory

Britain's Royal Air Force entered World War II (WWII) with outmoded and outdated aeroplanes, albeit with great designs in the pipeline. It had two significant technologies on its side: the invention of radio detection and ranging, later called radar, and the development of a layered air-defence system for the United Kingdom. Within 12 months it would be tested to the limits and beyond.

But first came the Phoney War over Europe. RAF Bomber Command began with leaflet 'raids' over Germany before it became clear that the Nazi Party held the country in its terrible talons.

In the spring of 1940, the first skirmishes over France showed that although the fighter aircraft and their pilots were up to the mark, the theory that 'the bomber will always get through' was misplaced, despite incredible heroism by the crews of the Battle, Blenheim, Hampden and Wellington aircraft.

RAF fighters were in action defending the Allies in Belgium, the Netherlands and Norway, albeit in vain. But it was in France that the main actions were fought – fighters defending French airspace and daylight light-bombers suffering fearful losses trying to stop the Nazi Blitzkrieg (lightning war).

The Battle of France culminated in the evacuation of Dunkirk (June 1940) where RAF Fighter Command fought hard over the Channel and northern France to keep the Nazi bombers at bay. The losses were high at a time when the United Kingdom could little afford to waste pilots and airframes, but the need to bring home the British Expeditionary Force was paramount.

Sometimes described as the greatest battle in European civilisation, there is no doubt that the Battle

The mechanical hero was the Supermarine Spitfire

of Britain was highly significant. Fought over the skies of Britain, predominately Southern England, between July 10 and October 31, the Battle of Britain demonstrated the British had the resolve to stand up to the German war machine, at a time when the rest of Europe was under the Fascist yoke.

It was a close run thing, but the British, through the foresight of Air Marshal Sir Hugh Dowding and the brilliant tactical leadership of Air Vice Marshal Keith Park, were well-prepared, if outnumbered. The RAF had a better training programme and the factories of Britain could replace fighter aircraft faster than their German counterparts.

Of course, the mechanical hero was the Supermarine Spitfire – a high-speed (400+mph), eight-gun, monoplane fighter – but more aircraft were actually destroyed by the Hawker Hurricane. The Battle was to have been the prelude to an invasion of the British Isles, but the Germans paused and lost the initiative. Hitler had other ideas – attacking Russia was an easier nut to crack, he thought.

Fighting back

Taking the battle to the enemy when the whole of Europe was in enemy hands, or neutral, was a key requirement of 1941. The Royal Air Force fought back with highly-organised fighter sweeps over France with the Spitfire, Hurricane and, soon, the Bristol Beaufighter. Radar-equipped Beaufighters also engaged German bombers at night but elsewhere the war clouds were gathering.

"The plane crashed and exploded"

"It was a date I will never forget". Air Vice Marshal Reginald Bullen was referring to April 19 1944 – the day the engine failed on his bomber. That was also the day he would earn the George Medal.

The 20-year-old trained in England and Wales as an astro-navigator in 1940, and in 1943 he was posted to Malta. "It was very different in Malta. There was such a community feeling in England – you could go down to the pub when you were finished. There was nothing like that in Malta, nothing to help you forget the seriousness of what you were doing."

On April 19 1944, Reginald was in one of four crews sent out on a mission to seek out and bomb enemy ships. The overnight flight lasted eight hours and the crew returned at around 3.00am, to a very dark airfield, under terrible weather conditions. When approaching the circuit for landing, he realised the engine had failed.

"The plane crashed and exploded. I was blown some 20 yards away. I don't remember much after that, but I'm told I went back to drag someone out of the wreckage". That person was Warrant Officer Wally Clarke of the Royal Australian Air Force. Out of the six crew-members, Wally Clarke and Reginald were the only survivors.

Eventually, Reginald was flown back to England for treatment in Bristol, but his condition made it difficult to travel. The explosion had left him with burns and he suffered from multiple fractures in his right arm, left leg and back. "It had to be kept rigid," he explains, "so they strapped a metal bar with three pads along my back and I was laid on the floor in the plane. Apparently that was the best place for me. We stopped on the way to England, but it was a flying trip of 18 hours in total."

Lauren Rose-Smith

The small island fortress of Malta is halfway between Italy and North Africa. In the early war years, both mainland areas were in the hands of the enemy. For months, Malta was subjected to horrendous bombing by Italian and later German aircraft. At first, only three Sea Gladiator biplane fighters were available for air-defence, but later Hurricanes and eventually Spitfires were delivered.

In North Africa, the Western Desert became another battleground where the Royal Air Force needed all the tactical skill that it could find. Again outgunned by

"We bartered cigarettes for slices of bread"

Jack Spalding was a wireless operator gunner for the RAF until he was wounded, when he was moved to mobile signals. He flew with torpedo bomber squadrons, which were particularly hazardous, as they had to attack enemy convoys by approaching at about 600 yards and dropping torpedoes at 50ft off the deck. They ran into fierce resistance.

Jack was one of the members of the RAF that helped decide the outcome of the battle for Malta and, therefore, for the Mediterranean, North Africa and WWII. Malta was a base for British submarines and aircraft preying on Axis lines of supply to Libya. In the spring of 1942, the Axis decided to obliterate and starve the base. Jack had to endure terrible conditions, as everyone on the island was literally starving. "I have never before, or since, known what it was like to be really hungry. We bartered cigarettes with our Maltese waiters for crusts of bread and these I would wrap in a piece of silk and eat last thing at night to help me sleep."

Jack made his final run (August 28 1942) to attack a large tanker off the coast of Corfu that was escorted by four destroyers. They ran into heavy resistance and were hit, and he got a piece of shrapnel in his eye. He was lucky not to be shot down and puts it down to his lucky rabbit tail that he always carried as a lucky charm. "I hung onto it like mad. On every takeoff your hand went to your breast pocket to see if it was there." They managed to get back to base where he was taken to hospital and recovered. He later learned that his tanker operation had been successful and the ship had had to be grounded to stop it sinking.

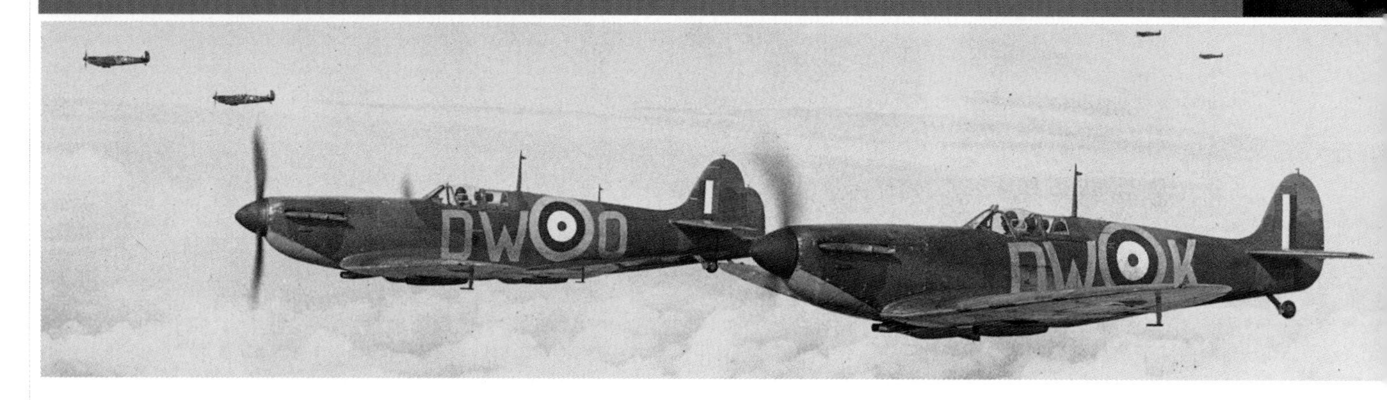

superior German types, the fighters, bombers and reconnaissance aircraft worked hard to establish air superiority, but it took time. It was not until November 1942 that Field Marshal Rommel's joint Italian and German forces were in full retreat.

Coastal Command also played its part in protecting Atlantic convoys from submarine attack and later took the battle to the shores of Occupied Europe, with strike aircraft operating from northern Norway to Greece.

Newly-captured airfields in Libya were put to good use by strike aircraft, including the venerable Beaufighter and the excellent Mosquito, operated around the Eastern Mediterranean, at times suffering high-casualties but always pressing home the attacks on Nazi fortifications, airfields, shipping and troop concentrations.

A cruel war

The main effort after the Battle of Britain was, however, the Strategic Bombing of the Third Reich. Nightly, from early 1941, the bombers would set out from bases centred in Lincolnshire, Norfolk and Yorkshire to pound the German war machine. First with smaller Wellingtons and Hampdens, later joined by the great four-engined Stirling, Halifax and Lancaster, the German industrial cities of the Ruhr and Berlin were attacked from the air.

Later, Mosquito-attacks carefully marked the targets for the bomber streams, but it was a cruel war, with crews often airborne for 10 hours in freezing conditions and at the mercy of enemy night-fighters, searchlights and anti-aircraft fire. The ground crews also worked hard to keep the bombers in the air. Some raids were especially famous:

Bombers would set out from their bases to pound the German war machine

destroying the industrial dams in 1943, 'thousand bomber raids' on Hamburg, Cologne and Berlin and, of course, the much-debated attack on Dresden in 1945.

Often forgotten, even before the end of fighting in Europe, the heroes of the Burma campaign certainly deserve their place in the history of the Royal Air Force in WWII. Thrown back by the superior Japanese air forces at the begining of the war, it was two years before the Beaufighter (dubbed 'whistling death' by the Japanese), Hurricane, Thunderbolt and Mosquito turned the tide and, supporting the 14th Army Group, threw the invaders from the borders of India and back through Burma and Siam (now Thailand) to Malay (now Malaysia).

None of this would have been possible without the dedicated men and women of the training commands, spread across the Commonwealth, the transport forces that kept communications going, even in the dark days of 1941-42, and, of course, the ground crews that kept the aeroplanes flying. ■

"We didn't worry about the bomb scares"

At the age of 20, Diana Lawford had few social freedoms and no experience of the working environment – until she joined the Woman's Auxiliary Air Force in 1942.

"It was a wonderful experience because I was an only child, very, very nervous, and going anywhere on my own was a major thing."

Trained in Lancashire, Diana was designated to the equipment section, supplying spare parts to Spitfires. She was soon transferred to Eastbourne and she recalls mixing with all types of people.

"Recreation was fabulous. We went to big dances with the pilots and sometimes shows from the West End would come to entertain us. In fact, we were having such a wonderful time that we didn't worry about the bomb scares. They were often at the edge of the airfields. To us it was just another air raid, and it was just as well because, if not, we would have been gibbering idiots." *Lauren Rose-Smith*

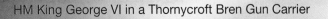

The biggest victory that women won was the battle for hearts, minds and spirit

Queuing became a way of life. When a shopkeeper received new stock, word rapidly spread

People at war

Unsung heroes

professionals or volunteers, the war years generated many heroes and heroines. By Richard Morris

The war placed large numbers of ordinary people in extraordinary physical and social surroundings. Some gave their spare time to the Air Raid Precautions (ARP), the Auxiliary Fire Service or the Voluntary Aid Detachment. Many joined the Home Guard, while police, fire-fighters and nurses found their peacetime roles intensified.

Least sung of all, perhaps, were stalwarts like miners and farmers whose work supported everything else, but attracted comparatively little attention, or those who simply carried on in the face of sorrow.

Heroism took many forms. In September 1942, William Foster was coming up to his 62nd birthday – an age when many would be thinking of retirement or pottering in the garden. Foster, however, had gained soldiering experience during the Great War (World War I, 1914-18) and volunteered for the Home Guard. The second Sunday that month found him in a trench near Salisbury, showing recruits how to throw hand grenades. A bad throw by one of his pupils caused a live grenade to bounce back into the trench. With no time to lob it out again, Foster threw himself across the weapon to shield the recruits from its blast. A second or two later the grenade went off, and killed him.

Another volunteer who took a split-second decision was Albert Dolphin, an Emergency Hospital Service porter who worked at New Cross. On the afternoon of Black Saturday – the warm September day in 1940 when the Luftwaffe launched its first mass attack on London – his hospital was hit. With others, Dolphin went to the aid of a nurse who was trapped by fallen masonry. Nearby, a wall teetered. As it began to fall, other rescuers stood clear, but Dolphin stayed with the nurse, using his own body to protect her from the tumbling rubble. The nurse survived; Dolphin died.

These were acts of unconditional love for fellow humans, for which both men were awarded the George Cross. The spontaneity of their self-sacrifice should not obscure the fact that they knew what they were doing – that the effect of adrenaline was to sharpen judgement, not override it.

Some deeds were sustained for many hours. Typical were the actions of the ARP and civil defence rescue services that laboured to release victims from bombed buildings. Many victims became trapped when buildings collapsed over the cellars in which they had taken shelter. In some cases rescuers burrowed through unstable rubble. In others, a shaft was dug nearby, followed by the boring of a tunnel through foundations. Later in the war, some teams used trained dogs to detect survivors.

Inherently dangerous, such work was yet more unnerving when an air-raid was still in progress, where the rescuers were overshadowed by the swaying walls of a tottering building, or where they were hindered by ruptured gas or water mains. Or fire.

On February 20 1944, Leslie Fox, a member of the London County Council Heavy Rescue Service, worked for two hours in a burning ruin, shifting rubble so hot that it could scarcely be handled, to locate and free a survivor.

Such efforts seem to have been sustained by a kind of passion – a furious, unrelenting spend of energy that went on until the victim was out or the fire quenched.

By contrast, the making safe of an unexploded bomb (UXB) called less for sustained physical effort (though digging down to work on one often did demand that) so much as judgement and calm detachment. Part of this was to know whether the bomb was unexploded because it was faulty, or merely biding its time.

Alongside blast bombs and incendiaries, delayed-action weapons were used to disrupt life and production by forcing neighbourhood evacuations, and to attract and kill those sent to deal with them. Some weapons were booby-trapped, using anti-handling devices that were periodically altered so as to outwit those who attempted to make them safe.

In December 1940, John Babington, a former physics teacher, repeatedly descended down a 5m (16ft, approx) shaft in Chatham dockyard to extract a fuse protected by an anti-handling device, in the knowledge that a similar device had already killed another officer. Lt Bertram Trevelyan was another whose resolve ensured that others would live. An architect before the war, Trevelyan dealt with hundreds of unexploded bombs, and neutralised six hitherto unknown fuse types.

A number of conscientious objectors worked in bomb disposal, making the point that an unwillingness to fight might be a moral matter that did not necessarily have anything to do with a lack of courage.

Superhumans

The original sense of the Greek *hirȳs* was someone of superhuman quality. We begin to see how such a quality might gleam in historically unfamiliar ways: the farm-hand who stayed in the open during an air-raid to steady his terrified horses; the heroism of collective withstanding, caught by Humphrey Jennings's film *London Can Take It* (1940); the heroism of perseverance, or bereavement.

In these days when 'pressure' and 'stress' are traced to the least important things, it is difficult to appreciate the effects of the war's unmerciful appetite for lives or its demand for family partings.

For years at a time, almost everybody was separated from somebody and if the war didn't claim you or your relatives, it would certainly take members of a family you knew. In 1945, victorious Britain was also a community in mourning.

Hence, alongside the courage of ordinary people doing everyday things, there also grew a kind of personal fortitude of the kind needed to withstand the worst, and live through for tomorrow. ■

Blood ties

At least 2.5 million women were deprived of the presence and support of their husbands, serving in the armed forces

Separation, evacuation, conscription and displacement affected the lives of nearly every British family. Despite this, the family unit remained central to the 'togetherness' cultivated by a war-weary society and a country facing a mortal threat. By **Maureen Waller**

On May 8 1945, thousands converged on Buckingham Palace and cheered loudly every time the royal family made its appearance on the balcony. Not only was the royal family the symbol of national unity, but it also provided an example of unified family life throughout the war. King George VI and Queen Elizabeth were being cheered for their courage, their stoicism, for being there through the darkest times.

However, many ordinary British families deserved the same applause. The war had brought massive disruption to family life. It broke up not only families but also neighbourhoods. In Greater London, especially, there was wide-scale movement among the population, the less fortunate being bombed out and changing their address many times.

From the outbreak of war until the end of 1945, there were 60 million changes of address nationally in a civilian population of 38 million. Housing conditions, the separation of families and the effects of the mobilisation of women, were perhaps the most severe strains on the family in wartime.

Nationally, at least 2.5 million women were deprived of the presence and support of their husbands, serving in the armed forces. Many others found themselves separated from their families by being conscripted into the munitions industry or moved with government departments to other parts of the country. Family life was further fractured by the evacuation of women with children under-five and by the evacuation of children on their own.

The mobilisation of women was perhaps the most radical and disruptive factor. Traditionally, the place of a married woman was in the home, looking after husband and children. The government was initially reluctant to conscript women, particularly the wives of servicemen, in case it had an adverse affect on morale.

After 1941, however, the Ministry of Labour and National Service had to concede that it needed every ounce of the available 'woman power' for the war effort. Women

CHILDREN
are safer in the country
. . . leave them there
She's in the Ranks too !
CARING FOR EVACUEES
IS A NATIONAL SERVICE
ISSUED BY THE MINISTRY OF HEALTH

The once and future peace

"God bless Mummy, God bless Daddy, make me a good boy and don't let the war end. Amen."

I gabbled that prayer from the age of five until the Deity let me down in 1945, when I was nearly eleven. The pious requests were my mother's, who was supplicating the Holy Trinity to act as child-minder, and the last bit was my own, because I had worked out that peace would mean the end of my favourite wireless programmes.

The knowing innocence of childhood makes something peculiar of war. Lack of experience turns it into a bright game. The child is free to take what it wants from the mess; and the child is a callous animal, with little built-in morality.

For us, the past was something called Pre-war. It seemed to have been an age of milk and honey. Adults thumbed through old mail order catalogues and talked of the good days. If the past was Pre-war, the future had no name. We lived in a geological time span called the Duration.

The nearest I came to an understanding was that I was between two periods, of which adults were aware, but I could not be: the Eldorado of Pre-war, of which I remembered only the vivid yellow and the shape and taste of a banana, and a return to an Elysium after the Duration: a 'once and future peace'. I felt no sense of loss.

We lived a rural life beyond Manchester's suburbia, among the anti-aircraft batteries, and where the bombers jettisoned for the dash home. Heinkel? Dornier? It was the wah-wah of German engines. Then the guns. Out of bed and into the road to pick up hot shrapnel: metal with a texture like no other: steel sand.

Next morning in the playground we swapped our shrapnel and bartered for sticky incendiary bombs. Shrapnel that had been 'hot-found' was worth more than 'cold-found' though there was nothing by which to tell the difference now. It was a matter of unquestioned honour.

The Polish pilot should have been our greatest prize, but we lost him. His fighter was in trouble, and he crash-landed. He was dead when we arrived. We could not get the cockpit fully open before the fire reached the ammunition, and we had to leave his goggles and make do with a yellow handkerchief that was around his neck. But the blood was real.

Many city children had been moved back and forth in successive waves of evacuation

Our war was with the evacuees. We had them from Manchester, Liverpool, London and the Channel Islands. The Islanders were silent towards us, could speak a secret language among themselves, and would not go home. Manchester, Liverpool and London fought dirty, but were scared of woods and open spaces; so that, for us, a field was certain refuge from pursuit even if it was empty. The possibility of a cow lurking in the cropped grass was something that no townie would risk.

The adult plans for what they called the Home Front, (there appeared to be no Home Back; or, if there was, it did not concern them), were varied and improvised. My mother concocted the following stratagem against invasion while my father was guarding us from the Hun in Rhyl.

I kept a bag of pepper by the door, next to Mum's poker, ready for the German paratrooper when he knocked to invite us to surrender. As he knocked, I was going to throw the pepper into his face while Mum hit him on his steel helmet with the poker, and then we should run upstairs and commit suicide by hurling ourselves head first from the bedroom window. That the window was only some nine feet above the ground, with stone mullions that would have made 'hurling' difficult, did not make either of us question the efficacy of the scheme.

Peace came when a sailor gave me a banana. But it was green. He told me that it was not ripe yet. I put it on the mantelpiece and watched it every day. When it was the yellow I remembered, and the smell was as I remembered, I peeled and ate it in a Proustian orgy. At that instant of biting into the fruit, I knew that the Duration was over. By colour, taste, smell and geometry, a banana, for me, bracketed the Second World War. Then everything changed.

The Belsen films were shown at our cinema; and I saw them four times in one week. The not-dead corpse in the black skullcap, picking over his shirt and grinning at the camera that had come too late; the bulldozer ploughing its hideous choreography into the mass grave.

The Blitz, the bag of pepper, the dead pilot meant little. Belsen made sense. At the age of ten I realised what the fuss had been about; and I was violently wise.

Alan Garner

between the ages of 18 and 50 were at the disposal of their local labour exchange. Only women with children under the school leaving-age of 14 living at home, or who were looking after invalided or elderly parents, were exempt; in practice, a high proportion of these 10 million 'immobile' women – out of a pool of 17 million women between the ages of 14 and 64 – volunteered for war work of some kind. Part-time employment and wartime nurseries provided inducements for women with small children to do their bit.

A demanding schedule

Even though the hours could be long and hard, particularly in the munitions industry, work offered companionship. Many women relished the independence a job and a pay packet of their own gave them.

But they also had to cope with all the extra demands of wartime life: looking after the home and the children single-handed; making sense of reams of government bureaucracy, particularly if their home had been damaged or destroyed; queuing for food, juggling the points system, and struggling to make tasty, nutritional meals for the family out of meagre rations; valiantly trying to follow the government's urging to 'make-do and mend' and 'dig for victory'. In cities, they were also under strain from the bombing and lack of sleep.

Evacuation was never compulsory. Many city children had been moved back and forth between home and the reception areas in successive waves of evacuation, according to the intensity of the bombing. Their education had been badly disrupted.

Some children had had their horizons expanded by evacuation; others had been abused or exploited. With Father absent and Mother distracted or at work, it is not surprising that some children were running wild on the bombsites. There was a rise in juvenile delinquency, which the police attributed to lack of parental control.

In 1945 the BBC, newspapers and women's magazines were all at pains to offer advice to returning servicemen

War took its toll on many marriages

Another kind of fortitude

For 88 years Hilda has lived in the West Riding village where she was born – a place of farms, a paper mill, and a keen cricket club.

The youngest in a family of ten, in 1943 Hilda married David Pickard (pictured third from left), a sunny lad whom she'd known since childhood. David was a joiner, although by the time they wed he had volunteered for the RAF.

On July 28 1944, David's crew took off to drop arms to the French Resistance. Crossing the Normandy coast at low-level they were hit by ground-fire. David and the pilot stayed aboard the stricken aircraft while others got out, and died in the crash that followed.

In the same week that Hilda was told her husband was missing, news arrived that her elder brother's son Harold had been killed in the assault on Caen. Her brother himself died a few days later.

It was almost a year before Hilda learned what had happened to David. The wait was about the same length as the marriage. She has never seen the grave.

As a nation we salute the courage of those who fought. Another kind of fortitude belongs to those who waited, for the rest of their lives.

Richard Morris

and their wives on how to live together again. After so many years apart, it would not be easy. The men were shocked by the state of their wives. They had retained an image of them that bore little resemblance to the reality. Not only were the women older, shabbier and exhausted, but their personalities also seemed to have changed. They were more sophisticated and assertive, less compliant. For men thrust into Civvy Street with all its difficulties, it was unnerving.

Adjusting to post-war life

The dire housing shortage in bombed cities, where couples had to live with their in-laws or in sub-standard accommodation, added to the tension. Nor was it easy for the men to re-establish a relationship with their children, some of whom did not even recognise them from the photo on the mantelpiece and resented the stranger who was taking so much of Mummy's attention.

War and the problems of post-war adjustment took its toll on many marriages. Some marriages had been rushed, wartime affairs that did not survive the test of time; other couples had 'outgrown' each other, drifted apart or found new partners. There had been an alarming rise in promiscuity during the war. Loneliness and opportunity had prompted married women to have affairs. The illegitimacy rate was three-times the pre-war figure and a proportion of married women gave birth to children that were not their husband's.

The number of divorce petitions filed in England and Wales rose from 9,970 in 1938 to 24,857 in 1945, reaching a post-war peak of 47,041 in 1947. There were also about 25,000 legal separations in 1945-6, a 150 per cent increase over the pre-war level. There was also a spate of murders as gun-toting ex-servicemen returned to find their wives with other men.

For everyone, life would henceforth be divided into 'before the war' and 'after the war', so traumatic had the intervening years been. In a war that had torn families and neighbourhoods apart on a vast and dramatic scale, what is perhaps remarkable is not the number of families who were irredeemably damaged, but the social stability of the great majority of families, who perhaps grew stronger and closer as a result, and of the nation as a whole. ■

Clarrie and Beattie

Clarrie and Beattie Spence were married in April 1941 in Hull – a name the wartime censors changed at one point to a "North East Coast Town" in a bid to avoid confirming to the Germans that they were wreaking havoc with one of Britain's leading ports.

Beattie's father had died a few years before, so her brother 'gave her away'. He wore khaki and was soon to be posted to India. At the reception the guests toasted the couple with cheap sherry, but rationing ended any prospect of icing sugar on the cake. Instead it was covered with a lift-off plaster canopy into which the couple dug a knife to symbolise the ceremonial cutting.

The reception was short and so was the honeymoon to follow – two days south of the River Humber with friends in less-bombed Scunthorpe. They had talked of Torquay, but holiday and travel restrictions had soon ended that idea.

Like so many, Clarrie's war was not spectacular, but it was not easy. As a joiner he was in a reserve occupation, employed, among other things, fitting out mine-sweepers built at Beverley shipyard on the River Hull, a daily bike journey of 16 miles. A couple of nights a week there was home guard duty, manning a rocket gun on the East Yorkshire coast at Mapleton, a lonely clifftop village – so lonely that he was never ordered to fire one round in anger.

Then there were fire-watch nights patrolling the neighbourhood. Then the more normal nights – he and Beattie sharing an Anderson shelter with neighbours – one of whom, a redoubtable soul called Henry, used the air raid sirens ('the buzzers') as the signal to start frying sliced potatoes, sometimes known locally as 'scallops'. Defying the night raiders and the blackout, Henry would bring the scallops to the shelter, sometimes to the not-too-distant accompaniment of exploding bombs.

One night a landmine dropped on the nearby school field – its parachute flapping eerily in the wind. It didn't explode, but its impact with the ground shattered windows for many yards around. Another night the neighbourhood wasn't so lucky – a near direct hit on a shelter up the road killed an entire family.

It was only later in the war, with peace in sight, that Clarrie and Beattie decided to start a family. Their first child was born in a Hull hospital as the last of Hitler's incendiaries were falling on the city.

There were Clarries and Beatties throughout Britain – hundreds of thousands of them – making their contribution, making do, making home. All of them fervently hoping to bring their children up in a peaceful world.

ROCKET GUN CLOSE-UP

HERE is the first close-up picture of Britain's rocket-gun. The four pipes shown in the picture are in fact two sets of rails. The rocket is manhandled on to the rails and two rockets can be fired simultaneously. The rocket is almost the length of the rails and the whole apparatus is mounted on a swivelling platform.

In the years when our Country was in mortal danger

CLARENCE ERNEST SPENCE

who served 15th November, 1942 - 31st December, 1944

gave generously of his time and powers to make himself ready for her defence by force of arms and with his life if need be.

George R.I.

THE HOME GUARD

Name.... Cpl C. E. Spence

This card is sent to you with my best wishes and thanks for your services in the Anti-Aircraft Command.

With the rest of your A.A. Home Guard comrades you have been privileged to fight against the enemy in defence of your homes, and the effectiveness of that defence is a tribute to all your keenness and work.

Good luck!

F. A. Pile

GENERAL OFFICER COMMANDING-IN-CHIEF, ANTI-AIRCRAFT COMMAND.

Date.... 31/12/44

"We have just lived through several exceptionally intense months. At the heart of the commemorations in 2004 of the 60th anniversary of the landings and Liberation, and in 2005 of the victory, has been the Franco-British comradeship in arms, given pride of place through the most symbolic chapters in its history.

The message of gratitude and tribute to those who fought also sent a wake-up call to the young generations. Indeed the heroes' sacrifices remind us that the values they died for are just as relevant today.

Thanks to the "shared memory" initiative launched jointly with our British colleagues and friends, we shall be able to anchor the meaning of these values even more securely into our societies. We can see for ourselves the degree to which they also cernent the friendship between our two countries."

Hamlaoui MEKACHERA, Minister Delegate for War Veterans

"Nous venons de vivre plusieurs mois d'une intensité exceptionnelle. Au cœur des commémorations du 60ème anniversaire des débarquements et de la Libération en 2004, de la victoire en 2005, la fraternité d'armes franco-britannique a été mise à l'honneur à travers ses pages les plus emblématiques.

Le message de gratitude et d'hommage à ceux qui ont combattu était aussi un message d'éveil adressé aux jeunes générations. Le sacrifice des héros rappelle, en effet, que les valeurs pour lesquelles ils sont tombés conservent toute leur modernité.

La démarche de "mémoire partagée" engagée conjointement avec nos collègues et amis britanniques permettra d'ancrer davantage encore dans nos sociétés le sens de ces valeurs. Nous mesurons combien elles sont aussi le ciment de l'amitié entre nos deux pays."

Hamlaoui MEKACHERA, Ministre délégué aux anciens combattants

"The best way of paying tribute to the history of our nations is to work together to prepare for the future."

Jean-Pierre RAFFARIN, Prime Minister, 6 April 2004, to Her Majesty Queen Elizabeth II

"Le meilleur hommage que nous pouvons rendre à l'histoire de nos nations est de préparer ensemble leur avenir."

Jean-Pierre RAFFARIN, Premier Ministre, 6 avril 2004, à son Altesse Royale Elisabeth II

"You have earned our gratitude and our respect forever"
"Vous avez acquis pour toujours notre gratitude et notre respect"

British Veterans / Vétérans Britanniques

"The soldiers of freedom also came from the United Kingdom, a heroic nation that long held out alone, united behind its royal family and the indomitable Winston Churchill. A nation that, as the last archipelago of liberty, took in those who refused defeat and humiliation, those who carried the flame of hope."

Jacques CHIRAC, President of the French Republic, Arromanches, le 6 juin 2004

"Ces soldats venaient aussi du Royaume-Uni. Une nation héroïque qui a longtemps tenu seule, soudée derrière sa famille royale, derrière l'indomptable Winston Churchill. Une nation qui sut, dernier archipel de liberté, accueillir ceux qui refusaient la défaite et l'humiliation, ceux qui portaient la flamme de l'espoir."

Jacques CHIRAC, Président de la République, Arromanches, 6th june 2004

Women's work

The role of women in society altered considerably with the absence of many male family members. Women became guardians of the home front, as wartime necessity dictated that they took over the traditional male role of provider, explains **Peri Hope Langdale**

With the declaration of war in 1939, millions of men became heroes overnight. Willingly, they put King and country before their own lives and went off to fight on foreign soil, knowing they may never see their families again. Fathers, sons, teenage boys who lied about their age, all had the same objective – freedom from tyranny.

We remember, with gratitude and relief, their courageous acts, fierce patriotism and enduring comradeship. World War II (WWII) heroes defending democracy live in our minds forever. Yet, most of us are totally unaware the war also created millions of heroines.

Women themselves did not realise the huge scale of their contribution. The War Office said their work was "in the national interest" but everyone understood they were 'filling in' for the men. Nothing they did was seen as having a lasting impact or shaping the future we are all thankful for today.

Seven million, one hundred thousand women participated in the war effort on home soil – far more than the number of men who went abroad to fight.

"Without women, we would not have won the war. Yet most women never received any thanks or recognition, let alone a medal," says Major David Robertson, Chairman of the National Memorial to the Women of WWII.

Women were crucial to every aspect of the war effort. They built ships, planes, bridges and made munitions. They grew food; nursed soldiers and civilians; they ran field kitchens in bombed out streets; worked as code-breakers or saboteurs behind enemy lines. They drove buses, trains and performed hundreds of jobs, paid and unpaid, willingly stepping into the most important roles left vacant by five million men.

Women who had never worked outside the home jumped into dangerous jobs after just a few weeks' training: air raid warden, bomb disposal expert, searchlight operator and armaments worker.

"I went out a girl and came back a woman"

Eileen Marks was an ambulance attendant in Liverpool during the war. She would wait at the Liverpool Royal Infirmary, helping out where she could and receiving tuition, until an incident was reported. Attendants would then be driven to the incident by the ambulance drivers – many of whom were taxi drivers, as they had to have a really in-depth knowledge of the area. The vehicles were canvas-topped and occasionally Eileen would have to climb on top to put out the smouldering roofs.

On her first outing, Eileen says that she "went out a girl and came back a woman". She says it was dreadful to see the devastation. "It was very sad for people, looking for their families – their homes destroyed. Mostly I just gave first aid and comforted people – they appreciated that."

Eileen used to get the underground to work every morning: "I had to climb over all the people sleeping on the platform every morning. Their homes had been destroyed and they took their families and their possessions down there to stay safe overnight."

Despite all this, Eileen claims that, in many ways, these were happy times: "There was more community spirit, we were all trying for one aim. It was dreadful to see places destroyed and homes gone, but people were marvellous".

Louise Drew

People at war

The biggest victory women won was the battle for hearts, minds and spirit

Jennie Harrison worked in a munitions factory: "There was one girl, ever such a pretty girl, who lost all her fingers. I saw others with parts of their faces missing because of a detonator going off."

To add insult to injury, compensation for women factory workers who lost limbs was half the amount paid to men. And there were heartbreaking jobs. In the first three years of WWII, more British civilians were killed at home than soldiers fighting abroad, as women and children were deliberately targeted in order to instil fear and destroy morale.

By 1940, nearly half of the population was sleeping in public shelters and millions of homes had been destroyed. Desperate grief, poverty and hunger, even lack of basic sanitation could have done Hitler's job for him but, instead, women urged each other on to keep fighting back.

A 20-year-old ambulance driver recalls being asked to 'find somewhere' for a cardboard box of fingers and toes. Members of the Women's Voluntary Service (WVS), mainly elderly, ran field kitchens in flattened streets, shoving hot cups of tea into the hands of survivors.

THE NATIONAL MEMORIAL TO THE WOMEN OF WORLD WAR II

The memorial is both an eternal tribute to the past and a promise to the future: that the contribution of 7.1 million women towards victory in WWII will never be forgotten.

Cast in bronze by the Nautilus foundry in Essex, it is 22ft high, 16ft long and 6ft wide. Around the sides hang 17 sets of clothing, hats, handbags and gasmasks, representing the hundreds of different jobs women fulfilled in the absence of men... and it symbolises the fact they left their new independence and skills behind, returning home when peace was declared.

The sculptor is the renowned international artist John Mills, a former president of the Royal Academy of Sculptors, whose mother worked in munitions. The campaign to build the memorial was launched eight years ago by Ack Ack Command of the Royal Artillery Association. The veteran female gunners raised £350,000 from the public. However, without a grant of nearly £1 million from the National Heritage Memorial Fund and the support of Westminster Council, the monument could not have been built. It was unveiled by Her Majesty the Queen, a former member of the Auxillary Territorial Services, on July 9 2005.

Picture courtesy of ITV Tyne-Tees

WVS 'grannies' – more than a million of them – were there to comfort rescue workers and nurses digging through rubble with their bare hands. The WVS personified the battle cry on government posters: "Your image, your cheerfulness, your resolution will bring us victory."

Women started volunteering to do anything, and everything, two years before conscription began in 1941. They queued up to do war work because they wanted to fight for Britain in whatever way they could. The Auxiliary Territorial Service (ATS) was formed in 1938 to supply 25,000 clerical workers, but in 1942 there were 217,000 – a force of highly skilled engineers, electricians and carpenters. Many went to the front line in France, while others manned anti-aircraft guns. Mary Pattinson, 79, says: "My brother was killed at Dunkirk when he was 18 and I vowed I'd get one in for him. I was 17 when I joined up; I lied about my age. My parents went barmy."

In 1940, the Women's Land Army (aka 'Land Girls') had only 7,000 members – but by 1943, there were 10 times more. Joan Pringle, 81, clearly remembers her parents' reaction when she announced she wanted to volunteer: "Daddy said, 'Nonsense! You're not going.' But when you're the youngest of four and spoiled rotten, you do as you like." A physically delicate teenager, she lived in a shed without electricity or running water and worked 16-hour days on a diet of raw turnip sandwiches.

At the beginning of the war, Britain grew just 40 per cent of her own food and the Nazis decided to starve the country into submission by bombing merchant shipping convoys bringing supplies from the US. In 1941, Germany's U-boats (submarines) sank over 300 ships in three months; that was the year Marjorie Atkinson, now 83, married a merchant seaman.

He went to war never knowing she was pregnant and when the baby died six months after birth, she didn't tell him. She couldn't bring herself to add to his misery: "If a ship was hit and men went overboard the convoy carried on and left them struggling in the water." She saw him only a handful of times in six years but she counts herself lucky: "At the end of the war, he came home."

Many factory workers had two jobs in addition to looking after their own children and would often care for other peoples' children too. They would do 60-hour weeks and then work in civil defence.

Marjorie was a volunteer fire-watcher with the job of extinguishing incendiary bombs that dropped like confetti on Sunderland: "You got a broom handle and knocked them out of harm's way – if they landed on a roof they could burn their way all the way down through the house. You put them out with a bucket of sand."

But the biggest victory women won was the battle for hearts, minds and spirit. When Nazi wireless announced: "The legend of British self-control is being destroyed. The population is being seized by hair-raising fear," the opposite was true.

United under Churchill, British men fought on the beaches knowing British women were digging in for a fight wherever they stood: in kitchens, where they baked Victory Pie; in living rooms, where they knitted and stitched scraps into warm clothes; in the streets, where they salvaged metal to build war planes.

"Mary's courage lay in carrying on"

Mary Matthews joined the Land Army a few weeks before the outbreak of war. Both her parents had died by the time she was 18, and when her brother was shot down and killed during the Battle of Britain she was on her own.

Mary worked first on a dairy farm in Sussex, where the greatest risk came from a Dexter, which pinned her to the wall between its horns, and her most alarming moment was not the Dornier that bombed nearby buildings, but the sight of the farmer scrubbing his false teeth under the pump.

Mary's courage lay in carrying on. In 1941, newly-married to Jack Humby, she moved to Nidderdale to take on an 80-acre farm from a house with no electricity or sanitation, lit by lamps and candles. At 90, her chief memory is 'incessant work' through days that began at 5.00am and ended at 9.00pm, for years.

Richard Morris

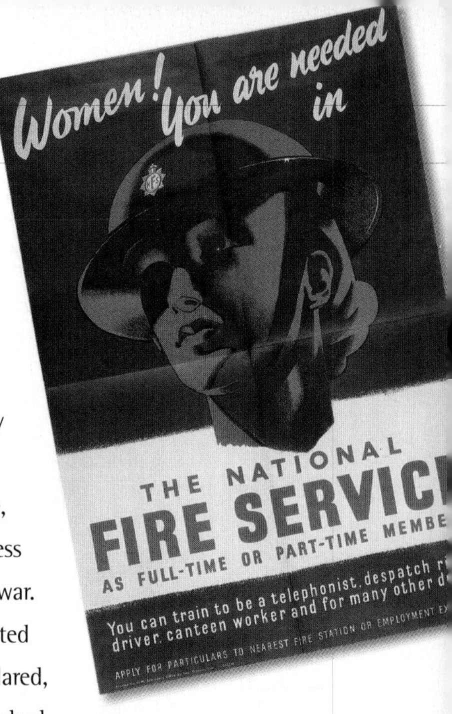

Whether it was eating indescribable muck, spreading it on the land or cleaning it up – they simply refused to be beaten. Resourcefulness, endurance, sacrifice and sheer cussedness were women's weapons of war.

But the government wanted more. When peace was declared, women were reminded they had been doing 'a man's job'; their wages, new skills and independence were borrowed privileges, not theirs by right.

Thankful to have their men home and the prospect of normal life, they quietly hung up their hats, uniforms and gas masks and left. Some kept their new jobs – at lower salaries than men – but mothers listened to government advice that children needed them at home.

It seemed to go quiet on the home front, but the seeds had been sown for the Women's Liberation Movement. The women of WWII joined forces with the younger generation, fighting for a fairer future. And now all of us are living the legacy of 7,100,000 heroines. ■

To the people who looked after the people...

During the war there were millions of unsung heroes – the people in public service. Those who stoically kept the country running under extreme conditions in the face of adversity. The people whose skill, commitment and sheer hard work kept Britain from grinding to a halt.

We would like to pay tribute to those people from the past whose dedication to duty is shared by today's public servants as they face new challenges in a continually evolving society.

To the people who looked after the people... thank you.

A schoolboy from Sevenoaks Weald Elementary School, the biggest juvenile poultry farm in Kent, holds on tightly to a cockerel trying to escape. Poultry farming was encouraged during World War II because it produces food efficiently and poultry clubs and rabbit clubs for children were encouraged by the Board of Education

Through the eyes of a child

"I think the trace of a tear appeared in my eye." This was the reaction of 12-year-old Richard Body (later an MP), on hearing Prime Minister Neville Chamberlain's radio broadcast on September 3 1939, announcing war with Germany.

On that same day, his mum and dad started packing. His father was a serving soldier and his mother had volunteered to be an ambulance driver. "A neighbour came in to shoot the dogs and cats," he recalls. From a large house in the country, Body moved with his mother to a small flat in the town.

Probably because of the absence of fathers and the closure of schools, juvenile crime rose by 41 per cent in the year after the outbreak of war. In the North West, the *Bolton Evening News* frequently reported crime, including thefts, burglaries, drunken and disorderly conduct, vandalism, attacks on women and 'blackout' offences. On October 10 1940, the Chief Constable complained about hooligans in the air-raid shelters.

After Dunkirk (June 1940), there was widespread fear of spies, and treachery. The 'pictures,' popular with adults and children alike, fuelled this and were important as much for war news as for entertainment. In *Spare a*

How did children view and react to the dramatic changes that World War II brought to their lives? What was their understanding of war and how were these views shaped? Those who were there share their vivid memories with **David Childs**

"We would hide in the cellar"

Ronnie Jacobson still clearly remembers the high-pitched wailing of the air raid sirens and the fantastical white searchlights that scanned the London skies, night after night, when he was a very young child.

"At first they tried to cover it up, as if nothing was going on. We would hide in the cellar singing songs to keep ourselves occupied and I treated it like a game. Looking back, I realise that was the most unsafe place to be, but it didn't occur to us then".

Like many children, Ronnie was evacuated, but was lucky enough to have family in Leeds, where he spent the rest of the war out of harm's way. He returned at seven years old to the street parties celebrating the end of the war.

"There was a strong feeling of euphoria, a real party atmosphere. Rationing was still going strong but everyone would join in and bake little cakes to share and sing songs."

Lauren Rose-Smith

As the war went on children learned new geographical locations

Copper (1941), George Formby uncovered a sabotage plot in Liverpool in which some hitherto highly respectable people were involved.

Went The Day Well? (1942), warned of Nazis in British uniforms and quislings in the local manor. In London, Geoff Robertson recalls as a teenager going to the Odeon, Clapham, when: "Quite routinely, a notice was flashed on the screen: 'The Air-Raid Warning has sounded.' The film continued; hardly anyone left the auditorium. Yet outside, at 10.00pm, the bombing was real enough. Shops in the high street had disappeared, ambulances and rescue teams were at work; people, presumably, had been killed."

Although the Nazis were identified as the main threat, many American 'B' pictures, like *The Purple Heart* (1944), exposed the fanatical 'Japs'. Children loved the American horror movies, for instance, *The Cat People* (1942), about a man whose wife believes, with reason, she turns into panther at night. Its sequel, *The Curse of the Cat People*, came in 1944. *I Walked with a Zombie* (1943), was also a great hit with children.

As the war went on, children learned new geographical locations: Warsaw, Dunkirk, Coventry, Crete, Malta, Cologne, Singapore, Stalingrad, Monte Casino, Arnhem and, at war's end, Dresden, Belsen and Hiroshima.

The involvement of relatives and friends brought more names. Dennis Skinner (later an MP), remembers Tobruk, Benghazi, El Alamein and later the towns in Normandy. He followed the war through the *Daily Herald* and played war games on the tip of the disused Clay Cross pit where Home Guard trenches had been dug.

(Professor) John L. Flood of Leicester, remembers the *Daily Express* offering its readers a map of the world with little flags to stick into it to mark the progress of the war. He grew very excited as the Nazi flags seemed to be advancing. With no television, radio was important for news and entertainment. Flood's family listened to the wireless and he still remembers the voice of 'the Radio Doctor' and that of John Snagge reading the news.

Others remember hearing the drama of the Battle of Britain (July-October 1940), the excitement of D-Day (June 6 1944) and the tragedy of The Battle of Arnhem (aka Operation Market Garden, September 17 1944) from the BBC.

The weekly *Picture Post* was another popular publication. In Maesglas, Wales, the precocious Leslie Thomas (the writer), whose dad was in the Merchant Navy, stopped having the comics *Dandy* and *Beano* and took the *War Illustrated* instead. As a 10-year-old, in December 1941, his mother woke him up to tell him that the Japanese had attacked Pearl Harbor and that the Americans were in the war. He replied: "In that case we've won the war!"

By 1940 food was a problem: one 'shell' egg a week, 2oz (50g) of butter, 2oz of cheese, 2oz of tea, 3oz of sweets per week, were the norm most of the time. "Tripe and onions, black puddings, liver and other nutritious offal made good any deficiencies in our protein supply, though we still queued for sausages, pork pies, cakes and other delicacies," remembers (Professor) Stanley Chapman of Leicester. Fruits from abroad were unavailable. From 1941 clothes were rationed.

Perhaps the lack of toys increased the interest in collecting other things. "Stamps, coins and foreign bank notes, much of which material originated from fathers and uncles in the services," recalls Chapman.

At the end of the war, returning servicemen brought with them Nazi medals, belts and, in a few cases, even daggers. Some boys felt strange meeting the givers of these prized trophies after years apart.

Some were disappointed that they did not say much about their experiences: the bomb aimer who said nothing about his missions; the Far East veteran who wore his overcoat in the house for weeks after his return; the engineering officer who had been on a raft in the Atlantic for 35 days; the RAMC doctor who had helped at Belsen. ■

"I didn't realise how serious it was"

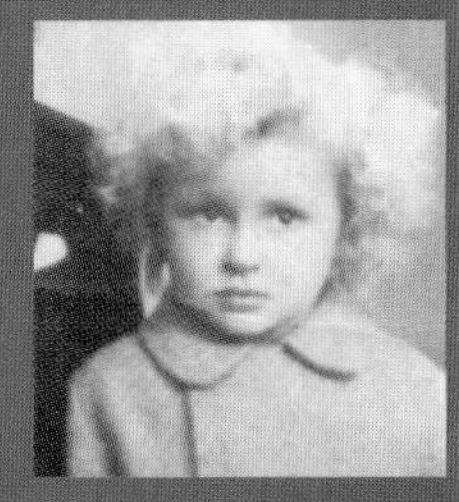

Patricia Ringer was eight years old when she and her family were evacuated from Upper Clapton in London to Spalding, Lincolnshire.

At school, the children were told they were to go on a trip to the seaside, and to bring a bucket and spade. It was only when they boarded the train at King's Cross that Patricia realised something was wrong.

"All of a sudden there was terrible crying and screaming. The women were grabbing on to their husbands because they weren't going with them and I remember someone saying war had been declared. I didn't realise how serious that was."

For the first night the family stayed in a derelict cottage, with only sacks to sleep on and a bucket toilet at the end of the garden.

"It was completely alien to anything we'd ever known. There was no electricity and, that night, rats and mice crawled over us while we slept. My mother stayed up all night trying to keep them off us. But the next day the local people donated chairs and tables and blankets. Generally, we were made to feel very welcome, but there were a few people who didn't want us around. To them, we were foreigners."

Lauren Rose-Smith

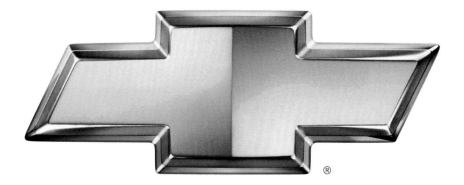

Vital connections

Hundreds of millions of letters passed between servicemen and their families during the war. Their carrying was an extraordinary undertaking, explains Richard Morris

During World War II (WWII), army postal services were co-ordinated by the Royal Engineers, whose system drew all mail through one centre, whence letters were redirected to provincial distribution centres, and on to individual units. From May 1941 this Home Postal Centre was at Nottingham, housed in a medley of buildings and premises that included the Trent Bridge cricket ground. Over 3,000 people worked for the HPS, where an experienced sorter would handle one letter every 3-4 seconds, and sorting went on round the clock, seven days a week, for four years. When US forces arrived they established a similar but separate centre of their own, not far away at Sutton Coldfield.

One reason for central handling was efficiency. Another was security, since information about unit locations could be used to monitor the movement of forces or forecast build-ups. To counter this, address details of servicemen and women were limited to personal details and unit names. Such 'closed addresses' were sufficient to enable the Home Postal Centre to direct mail to the places where units actually were. In the build-up to D-Day, outbound mail from members of invasion forces in forward marshalling areas was withheld until the invasion was underway.

Many served overseas. In Canada alone there were over 360 training schools that turned out nearly 138,000 members of aircrews. Others trained in the wide spaces of Australia, South Africa, New Zealand, and what is now Zimbabwe. Everyone had someone to write to.

Servicemen abroad on active service could expect to be away for several years without home leave. Dependence on letters was correspondingly strong. Conversely, a lag between writing and reading could cause anxiety. After May 1940, when overland routes to the Mediterranean were blocked, surface mail to the Middle East took up to six weeks – nearly four times longer than the average that had been achieved during the Sudan campaign of the 1880s.

The answer was the air letter – a combined letter and self-sealing envelope that was light enough to be carried in bulk by air. First used for communication with the Mediterranean and Middle East, the air letter was later extended to the Far East and transatlantic correspondence. It differed from the Airgraph, a system in which messages on a form were recorded photographically and transported in batches as negatives.

Montgomery believed an efficient postal service to be the single most beneficial influence on the morale of fighting men. Accordingly, postal units went ashore on D-Day.

Dakota crews made regular mail drops to troops fighting in Burma. The Royal Navy (which had its own postal system) organised the distribution of mail to crews aboard ships that were themselves moving around the oceans. Letters to prisoners of war went via the GPO to neutral nations, whence the International Red Cross took them on to camps in Germany, Italy and central Europe, and to the Far East. Letters from PoWs were often written in the tiniest script, to pack the most words onto small pieces of paper. Some correspondents adopted schemes of numbering, to identify letters received out of sequence or lost when ships sank. But no-one knew when separation would end, and there was a limit to how much could be committed to a letter that might never arrive. Many relationships broke down.

Wartime letters had meaning not simply as containers for news, but as proxies for those who sent them. Letters were kept, touched, and re-read. In 1945 they were quietly gathered in numberless quantities, put in boxes, and stowed in cupboards and attics. A lot of them are still there. Their stories are half humdrum, half Homeric, and most of them still await the telling. ■

Below are extracts from two sequences of letters. Many of the letters are long and richly descriptive, and these quotations give but an inkling of their range. One series ends in reunion, the other in tragedy.

John and Elsie

John was the son of working-class Londoners. When war began, he joined the RAF and was sent for navigator training in Canada. He met Elsie, a drama teacher whose family had emigrated from England in 1926. In 1944 John returned to England, and letter-writing began. They had resolved to marry after the war. They wrote to each other two or three times a week. In September 1944, John's flying training resumed, at a refresher unit in Wales, where for the first time in two years he had a room to himself.

"Yesterday was my day off and I went with a friend to St David's, the birthplace of the Patron Saint of Wales. The Cathedral there… is full of age and ghosts… I made up my mind to go there again; that visit may be years hence but then, please God, you will be with me."

After Germany's surrender the RAF hinted that they might have more work for him, presumably in the Far East. He told Elsie:

"…Even if we never met here again, there was reason for us to be the happiest people in the world. There is a deep reason for saying things over again to someone; it is that in the reiteration things may be known and understood all over again… It is the deep secret of rebirth; it is why music can be enjoyed twice over; it is why there is no end to love and no end to life."

John's 213th, and last, letter was written on April 9 1946, two years after they'd parted. Elsie was about to return to the England she had left 20 years earlier. He walked from Worcestershire down to the Wye Valley.

"Coming across the Malvern Hills, I first thought that that there you and I would come. I marked a spot high, untroubled and in deep solitude where you and I will rest after a long climb; and then that sense of being at peace and alone… The most lovely thing is that they were wishes so wonderful, so likely to come true. I have spent time on that thought, dwelt upon it unbelievingly… It has a been a long time my darling."

They married and 14 years later they visited St David's Cathedral, together.

Maisie and Stuart
In the late 1930s, Maisie Brownfoot and Stuart Campbell were students at Leeds College of Art. Stuart wrote to her whenever they were apart, about whatever he was doing. He joined the Territorial Army and June 1940 found him in the Royal Artillery.

"Busy digging trenches and moving the … entirely out of its field and into a nearby wood … for greater security from the air. We are now living like Robin Hood and his men in Sherwood Forest... On Saturday I shall be on special duty... It is a matter of staying in camp ready to rush into the hills and shoot or capture the German parachutists when they come".

Stuart's unit was sent to the Yorkshire coast on anti-invasion duty, then to Easington in County Durham. When Maisie visited, she stayed with a local family and brought her own food. They married on the last day of 1940, the Army allowing Stuart one day's leave for the honeymoon. In 1941 he was posted abroad.

"This is it then. We have been told to be packed to move anytime tonight. In the meantime we are confined to billets, which means that I shall not be able to ring you... By the way, I suppose you have heard about the Airgraph Service to the Middle East, you can get details at any Post Office. This will be the last time you hear from me for a long-time now."

September 28 1941: "It may be... that the mere sight of my handwriting will so gladden your eyes that you will be able to overlook the triviality of what I have to say. For between what the censor would cross out and what I don't care that he should read, I am reduced to imparting little beyond that I am perfectly well and safe".

At Tobruk, Stuart's gun crew fired until there were no more shells. He was captured.

September 3 1942, Prisoner of War Camp PG 70, Ancona, Italy: "I am quite well and looking forward to hearing from you soon. I hope you can let me have something to read, as I have nothing to do all day. The country and climate are like paradise after the desert!"

December 30 1942: "Well that was Christmas. I didn't do too badly, in some ways better than last year. Grand RC parcel with pudding, cake and sweets... I wish the mail was more reliable".

January 15 1943: "It is bitterly cold now, windy and freezing. We just sit huddled on our bunks and shiver."

February 15 1943: "I am completely kitted out now... The only thing which doesn't seem satisfactory is the non-arrival of my letters to you – I am still writing once a week."

July 22/23 1943: "It is known for certain that Sicily is invaded... Hurry up Montgomery." Then: "At last they have landed!"

However, German soldiers arrived and the stunned prisoners were ordered to move. A train took them to Germany

"The wretched story is to begin once more... freedom had been in our grasp for a week... How I love and dream of you... We have lost so much already – must we never have things our way?"

Stuart ended up in an industrial complex at Brux in Czechoslovakia, and set to work. On Sunday May 7 1944 Stuart received a parcel from Maisie.

"I hugged you for it my darling, the thought you had handled the things yourself was an intoxicating pleasure. You are the cream in my coffee... All the Elizabethan poets couldn't sum up the extent of my love for you."

Five days later, Allied bombers attacked Brux and Stuart was killed.
His diaries, letters, and some of his pictures survive.

Food for thought

Rationing was a fair way of sharing the food that was available, thus ensuring that everyone received a healthy diet. In fact, rationing had a profound effect on the nation's eating habits, as the poor and less well-off ate more protein and vitamins than before the war, while the better-off were forced to reduce their pre-war consumption of fat and sugar. The imposed diet, together with a more active lifestyle – petrol was in short supply, so everyone walked everywhere; plus, 'digging for victory' was also a form of hard, physical exercise – resulted in a dramatic improvement in the nation's health and fitness.

Customers had to register with their local shopkeepers and could buy rationed foods only from them. When buying food, the customer handed over the appropriate coupons, which the shopkeeper sent to the Ministry of Food (MOF), where they were carefully checked against the amount of food supplied. To supplement their ration, many people kept hens in back gardens and grew vegetables in allotments, gardens and even window boxes.

Typical weekly rations for an adult included: 4oz (110g) bacon or ham; 2oz (50g) butter; 4oz (110g) margarine; 2oz (50g) tea; 2-4oz (50g-110g) cooking fat; 2-8oz (50g-225g) cheese; 2-3 pints (1.2-1.8L) milk; 8oz (225g) sugar and one egg, if available.

Meat was rationed by cost, not by weight –1s 2d (6p) worth, per week – so cheaper cuts were popular. Sausages and offal were not rationed but were often

From early 1940, rationing transformed the eating habits of British families. With many foods unavailable or scarce, families were encouraged to 'dig for victory', growing their own food whenever possible and finding new ways of making the ingredients go further. By **Carol Wilson**

difficult to obtain. Household (dried, skimmed) milk and tinned, dried egg from the US supplemented the ration. A tin of dried egg contained the equivalent of a dozen fresh eggs that, when mixed with water, produced an acceptable substitute.

Rations for babies, young children, pregnant and nursing mothers were supplemented with concentrated orange juice, cod liver oil and extra milk. Obviously, the health and wellbeing of children was a priority. Hence, school meals were introduced during the war, thus ensuring that children received at least one nutritious main meal each day.

Scarce foods could not be rationed; as they were in such short supply the government could not guarantee that everyone would receive them, so a points system to buy these foods was issued in 1941. A monthly allowance of 16 points could buy a tin of meat or 2lbs of dried fruit, for instance.

Familiar trade-brands of basic foods, such as butter and flour, disappeared and were replaced by a single National or Pool brand to ensure consistent supplies.

Waste not, want not

The MOF issued an abundance of newspaper and magazine advertisements, recipe leaflets and radio broadcasts. These contained practical information to teach housewives how to make the best of what was available and make ingredients go further. Home economists were employed to demonstrate recipes in factory canteens, large shops and markets. To ensure that their families were well-fed, women, with great resourcefulness, quickly adapted to using new, and often unfamiliar, ingredients and cooking methods.

Women quickly adapted to using new ingredients and cooking methods

"Powdered milk sandwiches were a treat"

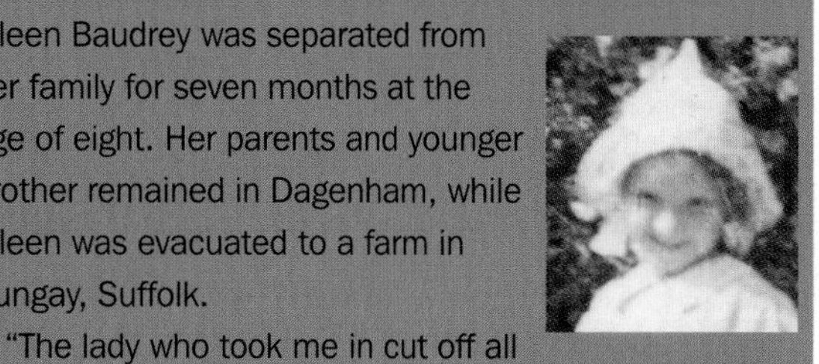

Aileen Baudrey was separated from her family for seven months at the age of eight. Her parents and younger brother remained in Dagenham, while Aileen was evacuated to a farm in Bungay, Suffolk.

"The lady who took me in cut off all my hair and washed it with black soap. I didn't like her very much for that, but she said it was to stop us from getting fleas. The food in Bungay was much better. We had fresh vegetables from the garden every day, so generally we ate rather well. Back in London I ate lots of powdered eggs, porridge and rice. Powdered milk sandwiches with lots of sugar were considered a treat."

Lauren Rose-Smith

Heroes with dirty faces

Neil Wallington celebrates the work of the London Fire Brigade and its firefighters during WWII

The men and women of London's fire service played a critical role in WWII. At times, the fire defence of the capital was under enormous strain, especially during the Blitz of 1940-41, but the resilience and determination of firefighters (dubbed "heroes with dirty faces" by Churchill) never faltered. Their endeavours and bravery is a story of selfless heroism.

Regulars and volunteers

Key to the UK's wartime fire defence was the creation of a nation-wide auxiliary firefighting force in 1938 to support fire brigades. The first recruits joined London's Auxiliary Fire Service (AFS) in the spring of 1938, and received basic training at regular London Fire Brigade (LFB) stations before being posted to sub stations in requisitioned premises. These recruits came from all backgrounds to form the 23,000-strong wartime London AFS - the pre-war London Fire Brigade (LFB) had consisted of 2,300 men.

The explosive and incendiary Blitz raids on London began in September 1940. From then until November 1940, London's fire service of regulars and volunteers endured 57 nights of uninterrupted raids. On many of these nights over 2,000 pumps were at work. While Londoners took shelter, firefighters worked on in the streets, rarely taking cover from falling bombs and incendiaries. They were constantly exposed to blast injuries and flying shrapnel, fire, heat, and smoke, and at risk from collapsing buildings. Night after night, most crews were weary, dehydrated, scorched, and covered in ash and dust. Conjunctivitis was common, as were painful body sores from permanently soaked uniforms. It was described in one vividly written diary as "unrelenting pyrotechnic hell". Each dawn with the 'all clear', firefighters would be damping down, and making up equipment ready for that evening's raids. Before the Blitz, the AFS crews had been derided as "war dodgers and loafers". From September 1940, London's firefighters were feted everywhere they went.

A national service

Following the last major raid of 10 May 1941, which ended probably the fieriest time in British history, there came a quieter period. In the interests of overall efficiency, the government nationalised the entire fire service. However, in 1944 the first V1 flying bombs rained down, soon to be followed by the devastating V2 rockets. For the London region of the National Fire Service, these brought new problems of firefighting and rescue which also often involved rescuing people trapped under tons of brickwork and debris.

Women at war

The women's section of the London's fire service contributed significantly. They were recruited from 1938 into a previously all-male organisation, at first for communications and canteen van duties. Once the Blitz began, women were soon pressed into front line service during raids as motorcycle despatch riders and petrol wagon drivers.

A heavy price

The men and women of London's fire service were in one of the most prominent home front organisations. The casualty figures bear this out, with 327 members of the London Fire Service (both LFB and AFS) killed in action, and over 3,000 seriously injured. Of London's 875 wartime fire stations, no fewer than 622 suffered bomb damage.

LFB
LONDON FIRE BRIGADE
making London a safer city

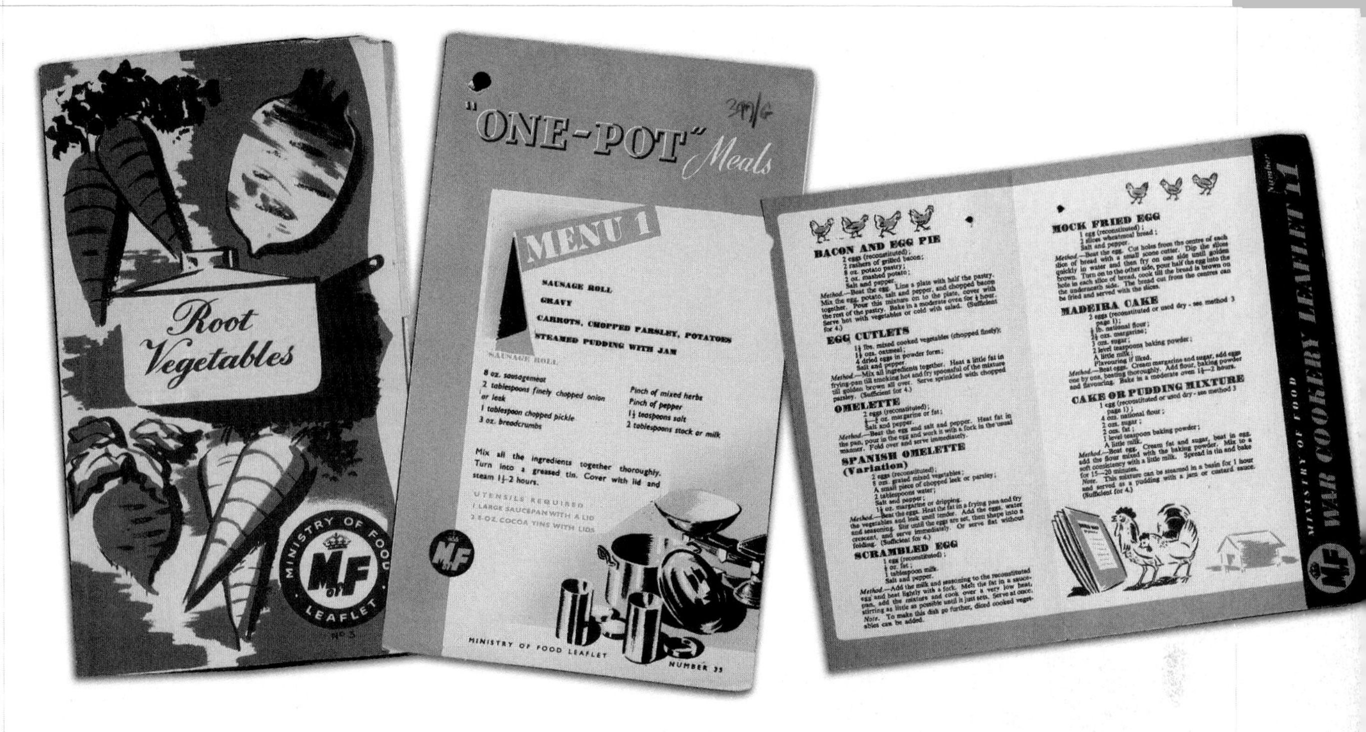

Queuing became a way of life. When a shopkeeper received new stock, word rapidly spread

Cartoon characters such as Dr Carrot and Potato Pete gave useful tips and recipes. A MOF leaflet, *Green Vegetables*, exhorted the public to eat a salad every day (when in season), plus plenty of cooked green vegetables for vitamin C, and stressed the importance of preparing and cooking vegetables correctly to retain their vitamins.

The famous Woolton Pie (a vegetable pie with nourishing oatmeal, topped with pastry or mashed potatoes) was named after Lord Woolton, the Minister of Food from 1940-1943. A former social worker from Liverpool, Woolton took his job very seriously and was popular with the public as he travelled round the country, giving talks and attending cookery demonstrations.

Cakes were a treat but the government recognised that they helped to make meals more enjoyable. Consequently, the MOF created recipes for cakes made with saccharine instead of sugar; with oats and barley to eke out the wheat flour; while 'dripping' (the residue fat from roasted or fried meats) substituted margarine or butter.

Indeed, some wartime substitutes are familiar ingredients today: the inherent natural sweetness of carrots, parsnips and beetroot made them ideal for cakes, puddings, tarts and preserves. Mock apricot flan had a filling of grated carrots, almond essence and a few spoonfuls of plum jam. Christmas recipes included an egg-less Christmas pudding, mock marzipan and a substitute for mincemeat: grated apple mixed with spices and dried fruits.

Food was precious, so nothing was wasted. Vegetable trimmings and their cooking-water, along with bacon rinds, went into the soup pot, and meat bones were used to make stock. Stale bread was crumbled and used to make savoury and sweet puddings. Milk bottles were rinsed out with water and the liquid used to make batters. Milk or water was beaten into butter to eke out the ration. And to feed pigs, local councils collected kitchen scraps. In the fruit-growing regions, groups of women gathered in school kitchens to make preserves

"Have ya got ya rations?"

Growing up in the country, the daughter of a farmer, it was natural that Olive Notley would 'do her bit' in the Women's Land Army. After training at the National Agricultural College, Sparsholt, near Winchester, Olive was posted to the watercress beds at St Marybourne, just 20 miles away.

"They told us that watercress is full of iron and vital for the war effort – especially for the troops in the Western Desert," recalls Olive. "As my half-brother Jack was there with the Royal Artillery, it seemed to me that I was doing the right thing." The work was hard and backbreaking, bending over the plants, up to the ankles in cold water for 12 hours at a time.

"Like everyone else at the time I was billeted on a family in the village." Olive remembers the greeting at the door on her first day to this day: "Have ya got ya rations?" Meaning, Olive soon found out, that her food-ration cards had to be handed over to the landlady and that she would be relying on her to feed her. Luckily, it was only for six months.

Paul Beaver

with specially supplied sugar. In general, fresh seasonal fruits and vegetables were bottled or dried.

Of course, queuing became a way of life. When a shopkeeper received new stock – for instance, a consignment of oranges – word rapidly spread and long lines would form outside the shop. On seeing a queue, people automatically joined it – even if they didn't always know what they were queuing for.

Creative cooking

Several recipes in *The Kitchen Front* booklet were from Poland, Russia and Denmark and were intended to add variety to the diet. There was even a recipe for chop suey. However, the success of the latter with the public is unsure, as it was made with whatever meat was available, carrots, green vegetables and covered in thick, brown gravy, which took the place of the traditional soya bean sauce.

Food manufacturers also did their bit by issuing their own recipe books. The *Stork Margarine Wartime Cookery Book* gave recipes for breads without yeast; cakes made with honey instead of sugar; along with a thick 'cream' for trifles, made from milk and margarine. There were also chapters entitled, *How to Save Your Dinner if Air-Raids Come* and *How to Make Wartime Food More Interesting.*

With everyone working hard for the war effort, meals needed to be filling and nourishing. In recognition of the fact that many women now went out to work, and to save precious fuel, communal eating was encouraged. Factory canteens, school kitchens and subsidised British restaurants served sustaining, healthy meals, not only to war workers, but also to servicemen on leave or travelling, and people who had been bombed out of their homes. In 1941, 79 million midday meals were served in British restaurants in just one week.

Rationing continued after the war, as supplies slowly returned to normal. It wasn't until 1954 that rationing finally ended and the British people could discard their ration books and buy their own choice of food again. ■

Safety first

Carrying a gas mask and observing the daily blackout were compulsory for each member of the British public. Despite the inconvenience, these rules fostered a renewed sense of self-awareness and neighbourhood responsibility among local communities. By **David Childs**

Germany was the first to use poison gas, in 1915 (during World War I, 1914-18), against the British and the French, who later retaliated. During the Rif War in Morocco (1925), the Spanish and French used mustard gas against the Berbers. Italy used it in its invasion of Abyssinia (1935). So it seemed likely that gas would be used in any future conflict, and the British government decided to give a gas mask to every person in the country, in 1938, before the outbreak of war.

In the basic mask, pieces of charcoal and cotton wool were put inside a filter. The filter would let the clean air through, but not the poisonous gas. There were several types of gas mask, including one for babies that was like a bag that an infant could fit into. There was also a gas mask for small children. It had big round eyes and a nosepiece; it was said to be like Mickey Mouse.

Audrey Chapman of Ilkeston, Derbyshire, has not forgotten the welcome interruption of lessons caused by trying on gas masks. This was done regularly so that children became familiar with them. "Guessing who was inside them became a favourite game and we were entranced when someone discovered that if you breathed (or blew) in them in a certain way, they made loud and realistic rude noises," recalls Audrey.

Most people who had a gas mask remember its unpleasant rubbery smell and a sense that one could not wear them for long stretches. Luckily, it never came to that. The police, fire brigade, civil defence and other 'home front' services always carried them. However, gradually, they were carried less and less by civilians.

After the war, the canvas cases used by the police and other services were employed by workmen to carry sandwiches or tools. For a time, women used them as alternative handbags or for clothes pegs. Indeed, prisoners in Wormwood Scrubs were still dismantling wartime gas masks in 1963.

Air-raid shelters turned out to be far more important than gas masks. Britain had been bombed in the 1914-18 war; Japanese planes bombed China in the late 1930s; during the Spanish Civil War (1936-39), Madrid, Barcelona and other Spanish towns were heavily bombed. The effects of these raids were reported in the press, in newsreels and by eyewitnesses at meetings up and down the country.

Fred Copeman, a Spanish Civil War veteran, who became a civil defence lecturer, remembered people fainting when they saw gruesome pictures of people killed in the bombing of Madrid.

Sheltering from danger

The government realised it had to act and Sir John Anderson, a member of Neville Chamberlain's government, was put in charge of Air Raid Precautions. For households with gardens, the government supplied 'Anderson shelters': corrugated galvanised-steel shelter kits. The earth that was excavated during preparation of the shelter site was used to cover the erected shelter. Free to those on lower incomes, higher income households were charged a small fee.

Some people were able to make themselves rather comfortable in their shelters. As Stanley Chapman, from Leicester, recalls: "In 1939 my parents paid for the building of a thick bricked, concrete topped, air-raid shelter in our garden; it was filled with bunk-beds and had an electric light and other comforts."

People got tired of going to the shelters, especially where no bombs fell, as Londoner Geoff Robertson remembers: "As the raids continued, you taped your windows with brown sticky paper, drew the blackout curtains and went

"The air was thick with dust"

Almost every house had a shelter in the garden, many dug in before the war to a national design, known as the Anderson Shelter, after its inventor. But if you were out shopping, on the way to work or simply travelling, you needed a public shelter. They were not always perfectly safe.

In Olive Notley's case, it was holiday on the south coast near Portsmouth that nearly cut short her life at 19 years of age. Arriving at the naval port of Portsmouth, Olive witnessed the first raids – 42 in 14 days – of the Battle of Britain.

The bombers that Olive watched on her arrival on the South Coast were the Luftwaffe's feared Stuka dive-bombers. "They seemed to hang in the air, then dropped like stones... I did not watch any more but almost threw myself into a surface shelter, where I thought I would be safe." But as she found out, the surface shelters were less than perfect. "The first few bombs crashed down into the street a few hundred yards away, the concrete building shook. But when a bomb landed within a few yards, we were blown off our seats, the air was thick with dust and we thought we were dead," she remembers today, with the clarity of a memory etched with fear. "I never went to a surface shelter again."

Paul Beaver

St Paul's Watch

For most of us it's hard to imagine life in London during the Blitz. From November 1940 to May 1941 the Luftwaffe poured a rain of fire onto the city. At its most intense, the sirens sounded on 57 consecutive nights of bombing.

Each morning, as Londoners emerged from their shelters to survey the devastation, there was one building they looked to for reassurance: St Paul's Cathedral. The great dome was the City's symbol of hope and defiance – while it rose above the skyline, the spirit of resistance was intact.

The fate of the great church was in the hands of 60 valiant volunteers known as the St Paul's Watch. Each night they stood guard in the Cathedral, defending Wren's 17th-century masterpiece from a relentless rain of incendiary bombs.

Fire bombs would burst into flames, creating an inferno that would engulf the building. The Watch was armed with little more than buckets of sand to quell the fire, and a scoop to carry the bomb away from the building. Theirs was a race against time to remove the incendiaries before they ignited.

Night after night the watch slept in the church – and night after night the sirens would sound to call them to duty. On December 29 1940, during a devastating raid on the City, Churchill sent the message that: "St Paul's must be preserved at all costs". That night, 28 incendiary bombs were dropped on the Cathedral, as the watchmen scrambled across the roofs to remove them. A black and white photograph taken during a raid shows the buildings around the Cathedral reduced to rubble, but the dome rising defiantly from the smoke.

That St Paul's survived is testimony to the courage of the Watch. These ordinary men and women are no longer here us to tell their story. But when you visit the church, take a moment by the great west door where a stone in the pavement bears the inscription: 'Remember men and women of St Paul's Watch, who by the grace of God preserved this Cathedral'.

There are bigger and finer monuments in St Paul's, but if it were not for the brave men and women commemorated on this simple stone, there would be no building for us to admire at all.

Marc Zakian

up to your own bed. A particularly heavy raid might force one down 'under the stairs' – officially recommended as the safest part of the house – with blankets and a hot drink [kept in a vacuum flask]."

Sometimes, however, the ultimate horror did happen. Aged five, Patricia Chandler was told that one of her best friends "had gone to be with Jesus". Her friend's house, at the other end of the street in Hounslow West, had been flattened.

Many people had no gardens and no shelters. In 1940, Fred Copeman was put in charge the public shelters for the City of Westminster and his first major problem occurred at Thames House, HQ of the Ministry of Aircraft Production. The two basements and the lower-ground floor were occupied by thousands of Lambeth citizens who had stormed the building across Lambeth Bridge. This was one of many occupations until some Tube stations and other places became available.

Tragically, many died while sheltering in some of these stations. For example, on March 3 1943, 173 men, women and children lost their lives in a panic incident at Bethnal Green station. Elsewhere, others were victims of enemy action. The blackout also caused accidents; 18 per cent of adults suffered some injury during the winter of 1940.

Yet, according to the Gallup poll, by October 1940, the Blitz experience was actually creating a new sense of community among the British people. ■

thank you thank you thank you thank you thank you thank you thank you thank you thank you thank you thank you thank you thank
you thank you thank you thank you thank you thank you thank you thank you thank you thank you thank you thank you thank you
thank you thank you thank you thank you thank you thank you thank you thank you thank you thank you thank you thank you thank
thank you thank you thank you thank you thank you thank you thank you thank you thank you thank you thank you thank you thank
you thank you thank you thank you thank you thank you thank you thank you thank you thank you thank you thank you thank you
thank you thank you thank you thank you thank you thank you thank you thank you thank you thank you thank you thank you thank
you thank you thank you thank you thank you thank you thank you thank you thank you thank you thank you thank you thank you
thank you thank you thank you thank you thank you thank you thank you thank you thank you thank you thank you thank you thank
you thank you thank you thank you thank you thank you thank you thank you thank you thank you thank you thank you thank you
thank you thank you thank you thank you thank you thank you thank you thank you thank you thank you thank you thank you thank
you thank you thank you thank you thank you thank you thank you thank you thank you thank you thank you thank you thank you
thank you thank you thank you thank you thank you thank you thank you thank you thank you thank you thank you thank you thank
you thank you thank you thank you thank you thank you thank you thank you thank you thank you thank you thank you thank you
thank you thank you thank you thank you thank you thank you thank you thank you thank you thank you thank you thank you thank
you thank you thank you thank you thank you thank you thank you thank you thank you thank you thank you thank you thank you
thank you thank you thank you thank you thank you thank you thank you thank you thank you thank you thank you thank you thank
you thank you thank you thank you thank you thank you thank you thank you thank you thank you thank you thank you thank you
thank you thank you thank you thank you thank you thank you thank you thank you thank you thank you thank you thank you thank
you thank you thank you thank you thank you thank you thank you thank you thank you thank you thank you thank you thank you
thank you thank you thank you thank you thank you thank you thank you thank you thank you thank you thank you thank you thank
you thank you thank you thank you thank you thank you thank you thank you thank you thank you thank you thank you thank you
thank you thank you thank you thank you thank you thank you thank you thank you thank you thank you thank you thank you thank
you thank you thank you thank you thank you thank y you th thank you thank you thank you thank you thank you
thank you thank you thank you thank you thank you nk an th ou thank you thank you thank you thank you thank
you thank you thank you thank you thank you tha u tha u nk y nk you thank you thank you thank you thank you
thank you thank you thank you thank you thank y ank yo ou tha uthank you thank you thank you thank you thank
you thank you thank you thank you thank youth you tha ank you k you thank you thank you thank you thank you
thank you thank you thank you thank you thank hank yo ou thank thank you thank you thank you thank you thank
you thank you thank you thank you thank yout you than hank you you thank you thank you thank you thank you
thank you thank you thank you thank you than thank you you thank hank you thank you thank you thank you thank
you thank you thank you thank you thank you you thank thank you you thank you thank you thank you thank you
thank you thank you thank you thank you than thank you you thank ank you thank you thank you thank you thank
you thank you thank you thank you thank you you thank hank you t you thank you thank you thank you thank you
thank you thank you thank you thank you than thank you thank you thank TM you thank you thank you thank you thank
you thank you thank you thank you thank you thank you thank you thank you thank you thank you thank you thank you
thank you thank you thank you thank you thank you thank you thank you thank you thank you thank you thank you thank you thank
you thank you thank you thank you thank you thank you thank you thank you thank you thank you thank you thank you thank you
thank you thank you thank you thank you thank you thank you thank you thank you thank you thank you thank you thank you thank
you thank you thank you thank you thank you thank you thank you thank you thank you thank you thank you thank you thank you
thank you thank you thank you thank you thank you thank you thank you thank you thank you thank you thank you thank you thank
you thank you thank you thank you thank you thank you thank you thank you thank you thank you thank you thank you thank you
thank you thank you thank you thank you thank you thank you thank you thank you thank you thank you thank you thank you thank
you thank you thank you thank you thank you thank you thank you thank you thank you thank you thank you thank you thank you
thank you thank you thank you thank you thank you thank you thank you thank you thank you thank you thank you thank you thank
you thank you thank you thank you thank you thank you thank you thank you thank you thank you thank you thank you thank you
thank you thank you thank you thank you thank you thank you thank you thank you thank you thank you thank you thank you thank
you thank you thank you thank you thank you thank you thank you thank you thank you thank you thank you thank you thank you
thank you thank you thank you thank you thank you thank you thank you thank you thank you thank you thank you thank you thank
you thank you thank you thank you thank you thank you thank you thank you thank you thank you thank you thank you thank you
thank you thank you thank you thank you thank you thank you thank you thank you thank you thank you thank you thank you thank
you thank you thank you thank you thank you thank you thank you thank you thank you thank you thank you thank you thank you
thank you thank you thank you thank you thank you thank you thank you thank you thank you thank you thank you thank you thank
you thank you thank you thank you thank you thank you thank you thank you thank you thank you thank you thank you thank you
thank you thank you thank you thank you thank you thank you thank you thank you thank you thank you thank you thank you thank
you thank you thank you thank you thank you thank you thank you thank you thank you thank you thank you thank you thank you
thank you thank you thank you thank you thank you thank you thank you thank you thank you thank you thank you thank you thank
you thank you thank you thank you thank you thank you thank you thank you thank you thank you thank you thank you thank you
thank you thank you thank you thank you thank you thank you thank you thank you thank you thank you thank you thank you thank
you thank you thank you thank you thank you thank you thank you thank you thank you thank you thank you thank you thank you
thank you thank you thank you thank you thank you thank you thank you thank you thank you thank you thank you thank you thank
you thank you thank you thank you thank you thank you thank you thank you thank you thank you thank you thank you thank you
thank you thank you thank you thank you thank you thank you thank you thank you thank you thank you thank you thank you thank
you thank you thank you thank you thank you thank you thank you thank you thank you thank you thank you thank you thank you
thank you thank you thank you thank you thank you thank you. **From each and everyone of McDonald's 73,000 UK employees. Thank you.**

Learning the hard way

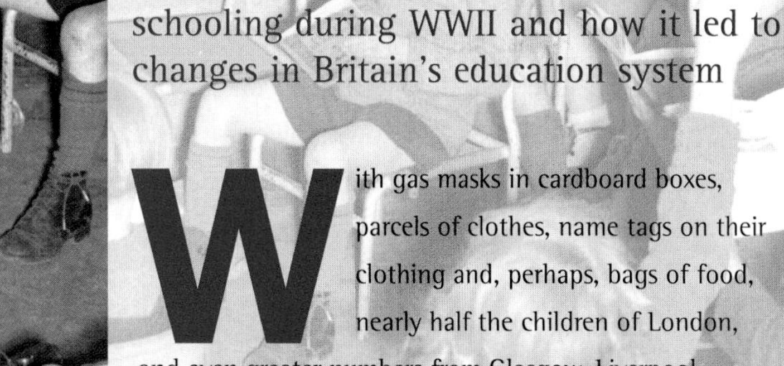

David Childs looks at the disruption to schooling during WWII and how it led to changes in Britain's education system

With gas masks in cardboard boxes, parcels of clothes, name tags on their clothing and, perhaps, bags of food, nearly half the children of London, and even greater numbers from Glasgow, Liverpool, Manchester, Newcastle, and some other towns, waited patiently on railway platforms.

It was September 1 1939. A massive evacuation of children, the under-fives with their mothers, was underway. Before war broke out, plans had been drawn up for this voluntary movement of children from areas reckoned to be the most likely targets of bombing. In most cases their final destinations were unknown. These plans were put into operation in the build-up to the war in late August.

The ministries of Health, Transport and Home Security worked with the Board of Education and the local

Those who had been left behind found that they had no schools to go to

authorities to transfer children, expectant mothers (13,000 went), some old people and hospital patients to rural areas. There were no reports of deaths or injuries. It was a fine, sunny day. Some cried, many thought of it as a great adventure. Even for many older children it was their first train ride and their first experience away from home.

Those who had been left behind found that they had no schools to go to, though a small number of teachers held classes in their homes for tiny groups of pupils. The local authority schools had been closed to make way for troops, storage of supplies, civil defence, and so on.

Schooling was also precarious for those who had reached the rural areas. There were just not the places and in many areas a shift system was introduced. Some resented the newcomers, some were dismayed to see how poorly clothed they were. Liverpool became known as Plimsoll City because so many of its children were sent forth in smelly rubber-soled, canvas gym shoes, inadequate for life in the country.

Children from Liverpool and elsewhere were infested with nits. It was not until April 1940 that compulsory education was reintroduced, but schools along the east and south coasts, the likely targets for enemy invasion forces, remained closed.

When, in 1939, the Nazi bombers failed to appear, many evacuees returned home, only to be evacuated again in 1940-41 during the Blitz. All this added to the turmoil in the school system.

Joe Ashton, later an MP, was evacuated to Leicestershire, along with his school. He recalls: "I got fed up with the countryside and returned home after a couple of weeks." Back home in Sheffield, he was bombed out and missed six months' schooling. Apart from one day a week, the time was spent "in glorious exploration of burnt-out houses and heaped chaos".

"Fear didn't come into it at that age"

The ships at Clyde Bank could be seen from the top of a hill on the south side of Glasgow, where Fergus Robertson was brought up. When his father, Jack, returned home for short intervals, the four-year-old would walk up the hill with him to watch the Germans drop bombs on the city and its ships.

"I can see it now as clearly as I could then – huge blazes of red, yellow and bronze. We were so close we could see their silhouettes. I wasn't afraid. Fear didn't come into it at that age."

Lauren Rose-Smith

The war brought a greater determination to improve the education system

The raising of the school-leaving age from 14 to 15, as proposed in 1936, fell victim to the war, as did further educational development. About 10 per cent of elementary school pupils were being selected to go on to secondary schools. The rest either remained in 'all-age' schools or went on to senior schools.

One innovation was that the School Meals Service became fully established. This was partly because so many mothers were working in factories, replacing men called up to the forces. It was also due to reports on the poor state of children's health and diet.

In some schools, other nourishment was provided. Andrew Wood, a pupil of Henry Gotch Infants' School, Kettering, recalls receiving one teaspoon of cod-liver oil daily, followed by concentrated orange juice. The same spoon was used without being cleaned between recipients. Some school children got Horlicks or Ovaltine tablets.

Many of the school buildings in town and country alike were in a poor state due to pre-war neglect and wartime shortages. Typical, was the situation in Beeston, Nottingham, a growing industrial suburb. The largest primary school was in temporary buildings erected after World War I, while the old village school overflowed into the hall of a Baptist Chapel, 10 minutes' walk away.

Room for improvement

In many schools, class sizes often reached 50 or more while books were limited and out-of-date. The emphasis in teaching was on the 'three Rs' – reading, writing and arithmetic – with tables being learnt by rote. Geography lessons often emphasised parts of the British Empire, like Australia, and Empire Day was celebrated with fancy dress. All this gave children an unrealistic picture of Britain's true place in the world. Coping with these conditions were male teachers unfit or too old for military service, re-engaged retired teachers and women teachers, many of whom had retired on getting married.

Corporal punishment was the norm and some teachers used it liberally on boys and girls. Lateness, copying other children's work, talking without permission, fighting or 'cheek' commonly were awarded with several strokes of the cane.

The war brought a greater determination to improve the education system and this produced the Education Act (1944), which created the Ministry of Education. It established a nationwide system of free, compulsory schooling from age five to 15 (introduced in 1947) and secondary schools divided into modern, for the great majority, grammar and technical. In the post-war austerity, to Britain's cost, few technical schools were established.

Where few bombs fell, others remembered 'digging for victory' on school plots or collecting money for the Spitfire Fund. As German bombing raids were mainly at night, not many children were killed in schools, as Fred Barnes, an Eastender, remembers: "As a young lad I saw many casualties and deaths. The worst moments were when the school register was called the morning after a heavy raid... and no answer was given." ■

Bringing the nation together

In recent years UK citizens have joined together to celebrate national and historical events. Andrew Maiden profiles the company and its chairman behind some of those events

Beacon Millennium Limited is a company that is both visible and invisible to UK citizens. The name may not be immediately familiar to many, but the company's activities couldn't have been more noticeable to all since it has been responsible for a number of the biggest national celebrations in recent times.

The company was set up by Bruno Peek OBE MVO, a highly experienced and respected events organiser who first spotted the need for celebrations of national, historical events during the 1980s.

The first major project he undertook was Fire over England in 1988. This consisted of 400 beacon signal fires lit across England and Wales to celebrate the 400th anniversary of the sighting of the Spanish Armada. The Spanish Ambassador to the Court of St James was invited to light the first beacon on the Lizard, Cornwall. The event was subsequently described by *The Sunday Telegraph* as "the biggest spectacle of its kind this century".

In 1994, Bruno was commissioned by the Ministry of Defence (MoD) to co-ordinate a commemoration of the 50th anniversary of VE Day in 1995. Over 1,500 street parties were held and over 1,000 beacons were lit, the first one by Her Majesty The Queen in Hyde Park during a live worldwide television broadcast.

The following year, Bruno was commissioned by the Royal British Legion to organise a 75-mile unbroken chain of poppies laid out between Cromer and Great

Yarmouth. The chain of 3.5 million printed poppies ran through people's houses, pubs and hotels and raised £391,000 for the Charity.

The next significant event involved the lighting of over 1,300 beacons across the UK to celebrate the arrival of the third millennium. Amongst others the funds to produce the project came from sponsorship secured from British Gas and a Millennium Commission lottery grant. The series of lightings began in the Scottish Isles and climaxed with the lighting of giant beacons in London, Edinburgh, Cardiff and Belfast, with the London Beacon being lit on the Thames, by Her Majesty The Queen. The idea and the drive for the project originated with Bruno Peek. It took him and his business partner, George Rocke, nearly seven years to secure the necessary support.

The next major event for the organisation was a global party for the Queen's Golden Jubilee in 2002. Bruno and his company co-ordinated thousands of street and garden parties, and promoted the lighting of over 2,000 beacons throughout the UK, the Channel Islands, the Commonwealth and 17 other countries around the world. The planning for the Golden Jubilee took more than two years. However, the overall event represented more than just an enormous celebration. "We brought communities, families and people from 79 countries together in one common celebration, so I think we have achieved a real milestone that won't be forgotten."

Bruno is a member of the MoD Steering Group for the 60th Anniversary of World War II commemorations this year, with the proud responsibility for looking after the Victoria Cross and George Cross holders on the day.

The national event currently occupying his company is the Trafalgar Weekend, taking place from 21-23 October this year, to commemorate the bicentenary of the Battle of Trafalgar. Individuals and communities throughout the UK and the Channel Islands are being encouraged to organise Trafalgar Day lunches, dinners and parties using local produce and regional specialities on Friday October 21 along with lighting beacons that night. On Sunday October 23 communities are being asked to organise church services of commemoration remembering the crews from both sides that gave their lives for their countries, along with ringing bells at 7.00pm that night.

For more information, tel: 01502 502626 (9.00am-5.00pm weekdays) or visit www.trafalgarweekend.co.uk

Special events

St James's Park

As part of the first Veterans Awareness Week, a Living Museum, Veterans' Centre and a World War II Military Vehicles display will be held in St James's Park from July 4-10. They will also be open on Sunday July 10 during the 60th Anniversary Commemorative events.

The displays will be situated next to The Mall and the public entrance will be opposite Marlborough Gate, roughly mid-way between Buckingham Palace and Admiralty Arch.

Visitors will pass through the security area into an avenue of stands where Veterans' Organisations will have displays explaining their work on behalf of the veterans' community.

The Living Museum

The Living Museum has been conceived as a place where the memories of the past can be kept alive and passed on to the young.

More than 28 Museums and organisations will take part to commemorate the lives of those men and women, both military and civilian, who experienced World War II. Visitors will be able to discover the experience of the war generation first-hand through real 'living' history. Re-enactments and hands-on displays will give them a glimpse of wartime life on the front line and on the home front – from air raids and black-out through gas-mask training and code-cracking. Visitors will be able to try on the clothes, pick up the objects, join in the songs.

More than 200 staff, including veterans, curators and enthusiastic amateur historians will be on hand to answer questions. What was it like to be in a jungle camp? Who 'manned' the searchlights? How did you put your gas mask on? What did the word 'spam' mean then?

All ages will be catered for with activities throughout the day. As well as large iconic objects, such as the tanks, planes and artillery on display, details of everyday life are on show. Visitors may also bring in unidentified objects (excluding weapons and ammunition) for an expert opinion.

The Living Museum is open from July 4-10.

Veterans' Centre

The Veterans' Centre will be situated next to the Living Museum and is a large centre where veterans and their families can meet and relax. Inside, there will be a refreshment area where veterans can buy snacks and drinks. They will also be able to watch a World War II light entertainment show from Combined Services Entertainment, the modern day successor to ENSA.

In the open space behind the centre, veterans can rest and listen to band concerts. The Veterans' Centre will also be used for veterans' receptions at lunchtime and in the early evening.

Military vehicles

A collection of World War II military vehicles from private and military collections will be displayed beside The Mall. The vehicles will be manned by experts who will explain where these vehicles saw action and what they were used for. They will also describe technical features and innovations introduced during the war years.

On July 10 the vehicles will parade down The Mall.

Images supplied by Royal Green Jackets Museum

Warriors for the Working Day

As part of the 60th Anniversary of the End of World War II, a unique exhibition of British WWII art called 'Warriors for the Working Day,' will be held at The Banqueting House in Whitehall from July 8 until August 5 2005.

This exhibition has been gathered from the Ministry of Defence Art Collection, regimental collections, service museums and other military and civilian sources.

The collection includes paintings, drawings and small sculptures, many of which were produced during or shortly after WWII. All the works will have aspects of WWII as their theme. Subjects range from major military operations at home and abroad, the aftermath of warfare, and the home front. Emphasis will be placed on the role of people supporting the Armed Forces, and the effect of the war on the landscape in which it occurred.

The Ministry of Defence Collection and Regimental Collections are usually housed in displays and buildings around the military estate. Some are kept in service museums, archives, headquarters buildings or military messes and are not normally seen by the public. Some works will not have been on general public display previously.

The exhibition will be held in the Undercroft of the Banqueting House, Whitehall, London SW1A 2ER. It will be open from 10.00am to 5.00pm, Monday to Saturday. Entrance is free of charge.

Sounding a warning

By Prebendary John Scott

Before the German Blitzkrieg swept into France, Holland and Belgium in early May 1940, most people in Britain had assumed that World War II would be fought mainly on the Continent, as the first had been; by the end of the Dunkirk evacuation a month later, it was all too obvious that the invasion of Britain was likely to be the next item on Hitler's agenda.

The government had urgently to find some means of alerting the whole country to the immediate danger of enemy landings. They chose the one signal which would reach virtually everybody in the country – church bells; and on June 13 1940 an Order in Council announced that bells were not to be rung except on the orders of the police or the military. If they were rung, it would be as a warning of actual or imminent invasion. All ringing came to an immediate stop the following day.

From then until 1943 most of our towers were left unused and unvisited except where their roofs were used as lookout points by the local Land Defence Volunteer or Home Guard. The ban continued for two and a half years. It was not until after the Battle of El Alamein, at the end of October 1942, that a special exception was made and we heard the bells again; by then the German armies were fully committed in Russia, the likelihood of an invasion of Britain had almost vanished, and the news of the victory was known to everybody. In April 1943, service-ringing was once more permitted; a month later all restrictions were lifted.

Inevitably there had been losses; London had lost three rings of 12, including one of the country's most famous rings, at St Mary-le-Bow, along with two rings of ten, 12 eights and a six; Bristol had lost a ring of ten and three eights (with another two in Bath); Devon had lost two rings of ten and three of eight, and a ring of six so badly damaged by fire that they had to be recast, but at Plymouth, St Andrew's tower was the only part of the church to survive undamaged, and the bells were joyfully rung for services, which were held in a church nearby. Many towns and villages had lost bells, and in other places towers had been so badly shaken by near-misses that the bells could not be rung with safety.

Many ringers were lost, too, but as the war came to an end, 'demobbed' ringers came home and things began to return to normal. In the years that followed, the bellfoundries, which had hitherto been contributing to the war effort, set about the task of replacing many of the bells which had been destroyed, the effects of six years' neglect of belfries and bell fittings were gradually put right, and damaged towers were made safe for ringing. 'The Ringing Isle' was back in business. ■

Church bells will be rung around the nation at 5.00pm on Sunday July 10 to mark the 60th anniversary of the end of WWII.

PROGRAMME OF MAIN EVENTS – VETERANS AWARENESS WEEK

MONDAY JULY 4 – SUNDAY JULY 10 2005

During Veterans Awareness Week there will be various displays in St James's Park, including The Living Museum, which features scenes from World War II; and the Veterans' Centre where veterans and their families may meet. There is also a display of World War II military vehicles beside The Mall. The Living Museum and the WWII vehicle display are open to the public and free of charge. The Veterans' Centre is open to veterans and their families. The entrance to the display area is in St James's Park at Marlborough Gate.

LIVING MUSEUM

Situated in St James's Park near Marlborough Gate, the World War II Living Museum features a range of displays that illustrate wartime conditions. These will include exhibits on the Front Line and the Home Front, which will be manned by experts, many of whom will be in World War II uniform or period clothing, and they will answer any questions about the display and about life at the time.

OPENING HOURS Monday July 4: 2.00pm-7.00pm
Tuesday July 5-Friday July 8: 12.00am-7.00pm
Saturday July 9: 11.00am-7.00pm
Sunday July 10: 9.00am-2.00pm

VETERANS' CENTRE

The Veterans' Centre provides a venue where veterans and their families can meet, rest and buy snacks and drinks. There will also be a programme of World War II entertainment throughout the day, including a show inside the Veterans' Centre and concerts at the bandstand in the area behind the Centre.

OPENING HOURS Monday July 4: 2.00pm-7.00pm
Tuesday July 5-Friday July 8: 12.00am-7.00pm
Saturday July 9: 11.00am-7.00pm
Sunday July 10: 9.00am-2.00pm

WWII MILITARY VEHICLES

A wide range of World War II military vehicles will be displayed beside The Mall in the area of Marlborough Gate. Nearly all of them are privately owned and the owners will explain their background and history.

THE MEMORIAL TO THE WOMEN OF WORLD WAR II SATURDAY JULY 9 2005

On Saturday July 9, Her Majesty The Queen will unveil a monument to the Women of World War II, which will be a permanent memorial in Whitehall to those women who served with the Armed Forces, the Emergency Services, and on the Home Front. The Memorial will be situated in the centre of Whitehall just north of Downing Street. Whitehall will be closed and members of the public may watch the ceremony from the Downing Street side of Whitehall.

1.00pm-2.15pm	Public admitted through security checks into the viewing area on the west side of Whitehall.
2.20pm	Ceremony commences
3.00pm	Arrival of The Queen
3.01pm	National Anthem Flypast by Tri-Service Helicopters
3.30pm	Ceremony ends. The Queen leaves for the Ministry of Defence to meet women veterans of World War II

COMMEMORATION OF THE 60TH ANNIVERSARY OF THE END OF WWII
SUNDAY JULY 10 2005

9.00am-2.00pm

LIVING MUSEUM – St James's Park
The World War II Living Museum features a number of displays that illustrate wartime conditions on the Front Line and also on the Home Front. The exhibits will be manned by experts who can explain the significance of the exhibit and answer any questions about the display.

9.00am-2.00pm

VETERANS' CENTRE – St James's Park
The Veterans' Centre provides a venue where veterans and their families can meet, rest and buy snacks and drinks. There will be a programme of World War II entertainment throughout the day.

11.00am-12.00pm

SERVICE OF THANKSGIVING – Westminster Abbey
The Service of Thanksgiving to mark the 60th Anniversary of the End of World War II will be led by the Dean of Westminster, and the Archbishop of Canterbury will give an address. Also present will be The Queen and members of the royal family, senior politicians and around 2,000 World War II veterans.

1.00pm-2.15pm

VETERANS' LUNCH – Buckingham Palace
2,000 World War II veterans will attend a lunch in the grounds of Buckingham Palace. The Queen will also attend the lunch.

1.30pm-2.00pm

WWII VINTAGE VEHICLE PARADE – The Mall
World War II military vehicles that have been on display in the North Carriage Drive in St James's Park will parade along The Mall to the Queen Victoria Memorial and then onto Constitution Hill.

3.00pm-4.15pm

COMMEMORATION EVENT OF REFLECTION AND REMINISCENCE – Horse Guards Parade
An event of Reflection and Reminiscence will be held on Horse Guards in the presence of The Queen and members of the royal family. The event will feature readings, humour and music from World War II, as well as periods of reflection and commemoration, including a two-minute silence.

4.15pm-4.45pm

PARADE OF STANDARDS – The Mall
Following the Horse Guards event, 600 veterans' standards will be paraded the length of The Mall and taken into the forecourt of Buckingham Palace.

5.00pm-5.15pm

BALCONY APPEARANCE BY HER MAJESTY THE QUEEN
At 5.00pm The Queen and members of the royal family will make an appearance on the balcony at Buckingham Palace

5.00pm

VINTAGE AIRCRAFT FLYPAST
Vintage World War II aircraft will fly down The Mall and fly over Buckingham Palace. They will be followed by the Battle of Britain Lancaster, which will make a poppy drop on the veterans in The Mall.

5.15pm

EVENTS CONCLUDE

Images from the archive

By Sheelagh Barnard

Buckingham Palace can be seen as an emotional focal point for World War II, representing Crown and State and People equally. We are all familiar with the image of the Royal Family on the balcony on VE day, the crowds celebrating. It is therefore particularly appropriate that, by gracious permission of Her Majesty the Queen, the Palace is once again being used as a giant screen to portray images of World War II.

Permission to project on the facade of Buckingham Palace was first granted for the Golden Jubilee Weekend in 2002 and the same techniques have been used.

The story told is that of the people of Great Britain and how they experienced the years of WWII. Whether military or civilian, these are the people of Britain whose contribution we should commemorate in the year of the 60th anniversary of WWII.

All the images used are from the Hulton Archive, kindly donated by Getty Images. This archive is a rich source for photographs which can support the underlying theme 'The Spirit of the British People'. ■

Vintage aircraft flypast

At 5.00pm on July 10 2005, the skies above London will be filled with a sight never before seen, when a formation of vintage World War II (WWII) aircraft fly down the Mall and over Buckingham Palace.

Five sections of aircraft, spaced at two minute intervals, will fly over at a height of approximately 1,000ft. The aircraft are scheduled to take off from Duxford aerodrome as part of the Flying Legends Airshow, then head towards London for the flypast.

The first section of aircraft will comprise five De Havilland Dragon Rapides, led by Captain Lee Proudfoot. This aircraft originally flew in April 1934 and was used in WWII for passenger-carrying duties and for radio navigational training. They will fly in a 'V' shaped formation, signifying the connection with the VE/VJ Commemorations.

The second section of aircraft is loosely based on a maritime theme. It will be led by a Lockheed Electra, which is notable for being the aircraft type in which Amelia Earhart made her ill-fated attempt to fly around the world in 1937. This aircraft was flown from America to the UK to become the Admiral's Barge of the US Naval Attaché in London. It was sold to British Airways after the war. The two Avro Ansons and two Catalinas in this section were aircraft types that saw service in Coastal Command during the war.

The middle section comprises three Douglas (DC3) Dakotas. The lead Dakota is ZA947 from the RAF Battle of Britain Memorial Flight, and it currently wears the livery of No 267 'Pegasus' Squadron, which flew in the transport, trooping and re-supply roles in the Middle East and the Mediterranean theatres during 1943/44. The Squadrons's role included the re-supply of partisans and resistance fighters, behind enemy lines, either by para-drop or by landing at clandestine airstrips. Thus this third section has a close connection with the land battle and the ground forces.

The fourth section is a tribute to Allied Forces and consists of two B-17 Flying Fortress aircraft and two North American B-25 Mitchell Bombers. The B-17 was critical to the USAAF daylight precision bombing

A formation of vintage World War II aircraft will fly down the Mall and over Buckingham Palace

Andy Lowe

campaign and was armed with 13 machine guns, hence the name 'Flying Fortress'. Despite their high casualty rate, B-17s became famous for returning home despite terrible damage and were fondly regarded by their crews for this quality. The aircraft is a strong symbol of the USAAF Eighth Air Force. The B-25 was one of America's most famous aeroplanes and was used by General Doolittle for the Tokyo Raid on April 18 1942. The B-25 first flew in 1940 and was used mainly as a bomber, but also for reconnaissance, strafing and submarine hunting and even as a fighter.

The finale is the Battle of Britain Memorial Flight with the Lancaster, Spitfire and Hurricane and a planned drop of one million poppies from the Lancaster. The Lancaster is one of only two remaining in airworthy condition, out of the 7,377 that were built. PA474 was built in Chester in mid-1945 and was originally earmarked for the 'Tiger Force' in the Far East. It is also famous for appearing in the films *Operation Crossbow* and *The Guns of Navarone*.

The Spitfire has been produced in greater numbers than any other British combat aircraft, with more than 20,000 Spitfires built in 22 different variations.

The Hurricane is one of the classic fighters of all time. It was designed and built for war and was at the forefront of Britain's defence in 1939/40, playing a major part in achieving victory in 1945.

A fresh coat of paint

At the start of 2005, Catalina (G-PBYA), operated by Plane Sailing of Duxford, was looking in a sorry state. Its yellow, red and green paint-scheme reflected the many years it had been used for fire-fighting duties in Canada and the general appearance of the aircraft was poor.

The operators had intended to re-paint the Catalina at the end of the year, which would probably have meant that the aircraft was unsuitable to be included in the vintage aircraft flypast. The RAF was approached to see if it could help, but a suitable painting facility was not available.

Marshall Aerospace kindly agreed to the use of one of their paint bays and, in May, with the assistance of six RAF tradesmen, work began on preparing the aircraft for its new colour scheme. Preparing the aircraft for painting took six days and Air Livery plc were contracted to do the re-painting the following week.

On June 3 2005, the Catalina was towed out of the hangar, sporting its new white livery with US Navy insignia and looking magnificent. None of this would have been possible without the help of Marshall Aerospace, the RAF, Air Livery and Newsdesk Media Group, who sponsored the paint and materials. Catalina (G-PBYA) can be seen in the second section of aircraft in the flypast.

1945 2005
MINISTRY OF DEFENCE
COMMEMORATION
1945
WW
II
2005

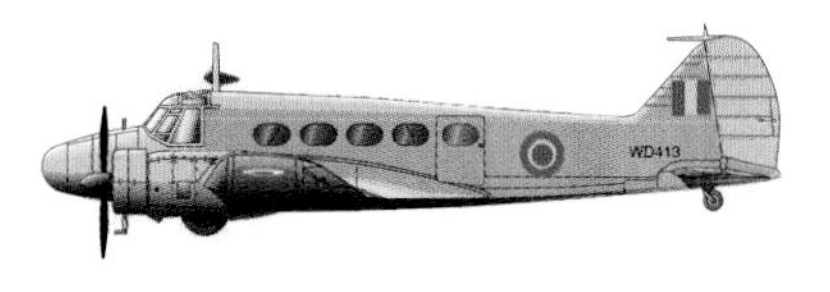

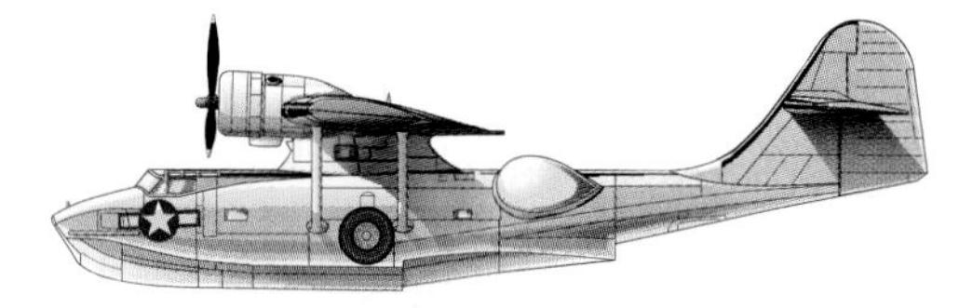

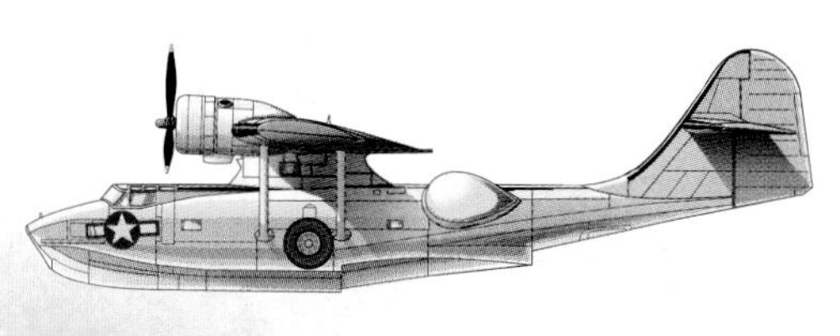

De Havilland Dragon Rapide 4

First flight: April 1934
Type: Transport
Length: 34ft 6in
Wingspan: 48ft
Maximum speed: 141mph
Cruise speed: 123mph
Range: 520 miles
Crew: One pilot, eight passengers

Did you know?
The Dragon Rapide 4 gained the distinction of being the first aeroplane to carry a reigning British monarch (King George V).

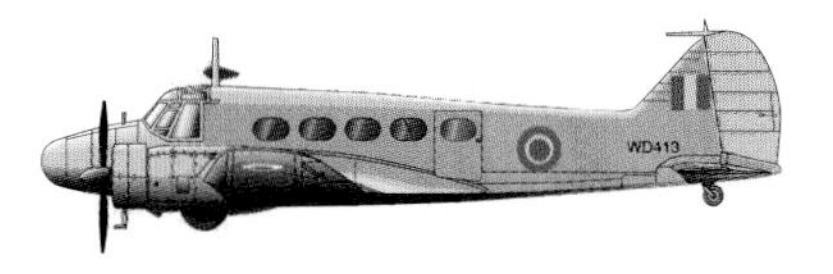

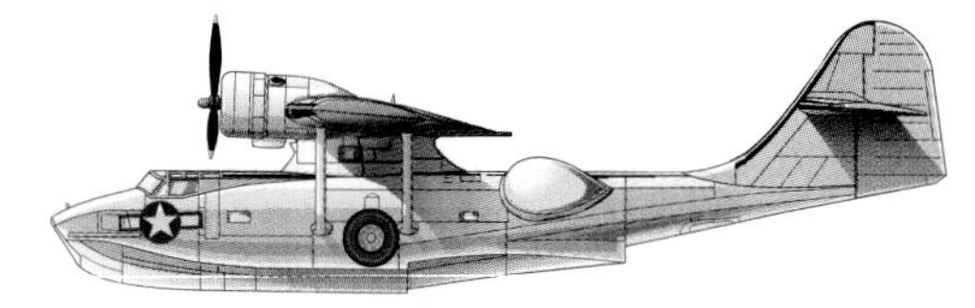

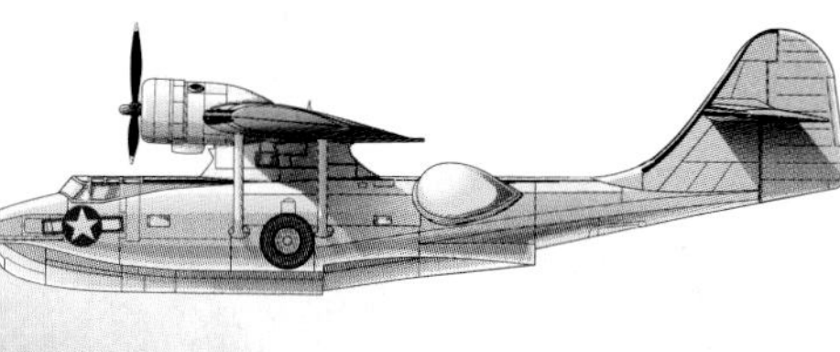

De Havilland Dragon Rapide 4

First flight: April 1934
Type: Transport
Length: 34ft 6in
Wingspan: 48ft
Maximum speed: 141mph
Cruise speed: 123mph
Range: 520 miles
Crew: One pilot, eight passengers

Did you know?
The Dragon Rapide 4 gained the distinction of being the first aeroplane to carry a reigning British monarch (King George V).

Lockheed 12a Electra Junior

First flight: February 1934
Type: Transport
Length: 38ft 7in
Wingspan: 55ft
Maximum speed: 202mph
Cruise speed: 185mph
Range: 810 miles
Crew: Two crew, 10 passengers

Did you know?
The Lockheed Electra is the aircraft type in which Amelia Earhart made her ill-fated attempt to fly around the world in 1937.

Avro Anson T21

First flight: March 1935
Type: Reconnaisance/search and rescue/training
Length: 42ft 3in
Wingspan: 56ft 5in
Maximum speed: 210mph
Cruise speed: 150mph
Range: 645 miles
Crew: Two pilots, up to six students/instructors

Did you know?
An Avro Anson made the first RAF attack of the war, in September 1939, on a German submarine.

Flypast

Avro Anson C19

First flight: March 1935
Type: Reconnaisance/search and rescue/training
Length: 42ft 3in
Wingspan: 56ft 5in
Maximum speed: 210mph
Cruise speed: 150mph
Range: 645 miles
Crew: Two pilots, up to six trainees

Did you know?
Towards the end of the war, Avro developed the C19 as an airliner. British European Airways flew some C19s on their Northern Ireland routes.

Catalina

First flight: 1935
Type: Patrol/air-sea rescue
Length: 63ft 10in
Wingspan: 104ft
Maximum speed: 196mph
Cruise speed: 107mph
Range: 2,545 miles
Crew: Two pilots, up to six crew

Did you know?
Catalinas flew with the RAF until the end of the war, and one sunk the last U-boat.

Douglas C-47 (DC-3 Dakota)

First flight: 1935
Type: Military transport
Length: 64ft 6in
Wingspan: 95ft
Maximum speed: 230mph
Cruise speed: 160mph
Range: 2,000 miles
Crew: Three flight crew, two cabin crew and 36 passengers

Did you know?
More than 18,000 Dakotas were built – some 300 of which are still flying today.

Boeing B-17 Flying Fortress

First flight: 1935
Type: Medium/Heavy Bomber
Length: 74ft 7in
Wingspan: 103ft 7in
Maximum speed: 287mph
Cruise speed: 210mph
Range: 1,100 miles with maximum bomb load
Crew: Two pilots and up to nine crew

Did you know?
In 1944, USAAF B-17s helped prepare the way for the thousands of troops who would storm Nazi-occupied Europe on D-Day.

B-25J Mitchell

First flight: January 1939
Type: Medium Bomber
Length: 53ft
Wingspan: 67ft 6in
Maximum speed: 340mph
Cruise speed: 160mph
Range: 1,865 miles
Crew: Four to six

Did you know?
The B-25 Mitchell became very popular in 1942 after 16 of the planes, led by Lt Col Jimmy Doolittle, made a daring and morale-boosting raid on Tokyo.

Lancaster

First flight: January 1941
Type: Heavy Bomber
Length: 69ft 6in
Wingspan: 102ft
Maximum speed: 287mph
Cruise speed: 180mph
Range: 1,730 miles with maximum bomb load
Crew: Up to seven

Did you know?
Lancasters were the planes that flew the famous 'Dambusters' raids on the Ruhr Valley in Germany.

Hurricane

First flight: November 1935
Type: Fighter
Length: 32ft 4in
Wingspan: 40ft
Maximum speed: 390mph
Cruise speed: 160mph
Range: 375 miles
Crew: One

Did you know?
During the Battle of Britain, Hurricanes were responsible for destroying more enemy aircraft than all the other defences combined.

Spitfire

First flight: March 1936
Type: Interceptor/Fighter
Length: 29ft 11in
Wingspan: 36ft 10in
Maximum speed: 450mph
Cruise speed: 200mph
Range: 450 miles
Crew: One

Did you know?
The Spitfire was very nearly named the 'Shrew', after its designer, RJ Mitchell, expressed dislike of the name 'Spitfire'.

NEWSDESK MEDIA GROUP
Flypast sponsored by Newsdesk Media Group
Aircraft details: Sean Maffett/Paul Beaver
Illustrations: jemsoar.com
Formation details correct at time of press

As well as limiting the impact of bad news, the media made the most of military successes

People are here to forget and to sing – just for a while

Make-do and mend

With materials in short supply, British people were forced to be imaginative and resourceful when it came to making their clothes. By **Lauren Rose-Smith**

Drab, simple and sparing – British fashion clearly echoed the austere atmosphere of World War II (WWII). The luxury of a full wardrobe and an outfit for every occasion became a distant memory as the war effort took precedence over the day-to-day life of men, women and children across the UK.

The new look was one of uniformity. Boxy jackets with large shoulder pads; straight, short and shapeless skirts; and sensible shoes all patriotically mimicked the soldier's attire. The new 'must have' for every woman was not a designer pair of shoes, sumptuous cashmere jumper or the latest silk scarf, but a standard sewing kit and plenty of creativity.

Making pillowcases into shorts, or blankets into heavy overcoats, was nothing out of the ordinary. Since it was announced in June 1941, rationing had generated a 'scrimp and save' approach to fashion.

With soldiers' uniforms and military equipment taking priority, the British public could no longer take clothes for granted. Many everyday materials were in short supply: metal buttons, thick leather soles and cosy woollen jumpers all started to disappear off the shelves. Thus, in order to take control and rein-in public consumption, just 66 ration coupons per adult were issued each year for the purchase of clothes, cloth and wool. By 1945 this was painfully reduced by almost half.

Put into perspective, a woman's coat over 28in long required 14 coupons, while a woollen dress took 11 out of the ration book. On top of the coupons, money was still needed to pay for the items and with the rising cost of material, many people found it increasingly difficult to buy clothes. The British population simply had to 'make-do and mend'.

A renowned wartime character, Mrs Sew and Sew, burst onto cinema screens, posters and leaflets promoting new ways of making old clothes last longer. She cheerfully demonstrated that patches could be sewn onto the elbows of cardigans, and worn-out woollen jumpers unravelled to be made into socks, short-waist cardigans and V-neck waistcoats.

No frills

The nation descended into a sewing and saving frenzy, attending evening classes that taught the techniques of converting your husband's trousers into skirts and old curtains into dresses.

All very helpful, yet, to poorer families, the so-called novel way of economising, and the fictional perfect housewife, portrayed a somewhat patronising image of a life of compromise – a life they already lived.

Nevertheless, Britain's citizens were determined to support their country and were prepared to stretch to great lengths to ensure they were not jeopardising their men and women in battle.

From 1941, pretty yet unnecessary frills, trimmings and buttons were strictly forbidden by the clothing order CC41. Utility clothing dismissed elaborate pleats and embroidery, elastic waistbands and fur trimmings in a drive to keep costs down and ensure everyone could afford good quality clothes.

Men sacrificed turn-ups, trousers had a maximum length of 27in (68cm), while only three pockets and buttons were allowed on jackets and the double-breasted blazer was thought to use far too much fabric. Even sewing and knitting patterns conformed to the legal guidelines, favouring open, lacy designs that used less material. As the

Eventually, the British public warmed to what was essentially a civilian uniform

war continued, the production line produced a variety of clothes so, eventually, the British public warmed to what was essentially a civilian uniform – a policy that continued until 1951.

It is easy to forget that while the world was at war, life at home carried on. Couples were getting married, sometimes just a day before one or both of them were whisked off to serve their country. But many girls refused to allow all the restrictions to get in the way of their 'big day'. Blackout material would be bleached, parachute silk and lacy doilies attached to create a dress as close to the one they had always dreamed about. Indeed, it wasn't uncommon for a wedding dress to be passed down generations until it was eventually made into feminine, frilly underwear.

Designers no longer had the freedom or opulence of experimentation with generous fabrics, and the rules and

Where there was a will, there was a way

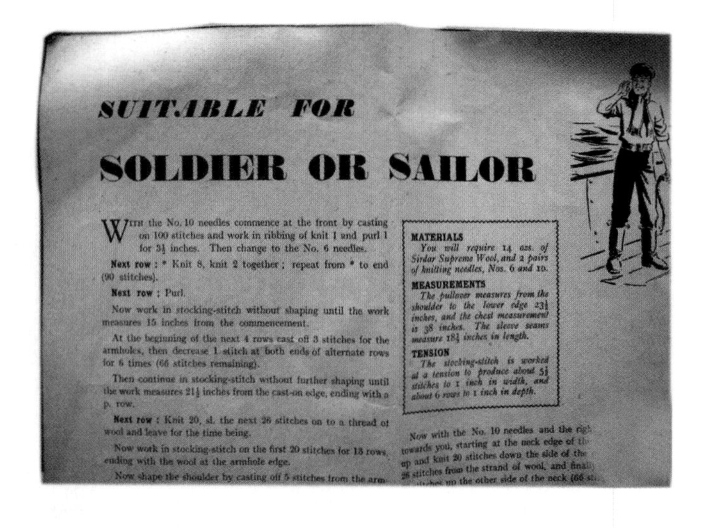

SUITABLE FOR

SOLDIER OR SAILOR

With the No. 10 needles commence at the front by casting on 100 stitches and work in ribbing of knit 1 and purl 1 for 3½ inches. Then change to the No. 6 needles.

Next row: * Knit 8, knit 2 together; repeat from * to end (90 stitches).

Next row: Purl.

Now work in stocking-stitch without shaping until the work measures 15 inches from the commencement.

At the beginning of the next 4 rows cast off 3 stitches for the armholes, then decrease 1 stitch at both ends of alternate rows for 6 times (66 stitches remaining).

Then continue in stocking-stitch without further shaping until the work measures 21½ inches from the cast-on edge, ending with a p. row.

Next row: Knit 20, sl. the next 26 stitches on to a thread of wool and leave for the time being.

Now work in stocking-stitch on the first 20 stitches for 13 rows, ending with the wool at the armhole edge.

MATERIALS
You will require 14 ozs. of Sirdar Supreme Wool, and 2 pairs of knitting needles, Nos. 6 and 10.

MEASUREMENTS
The pullover measures from the shoulder to the lower edge 23½ inches, and the chest measurement is 38 inches. The sleeve seams measure 18½ inches in length.

TENSION
The stocking-stitch is worked at a tension to produce about 5½ stitches to 1 inch in width, and about 6 rows to 1 inch in depth.

regulations might suggest the people of WWII were forced to disregard fashion completely. However, the war generated its own fashion – developed out of practicality.

Inventive solutions

The 1940s saw the popularisation of wedged shoes, where cork was used to create thick and sturdy soles instead of precious leather. Wedges were strong and comfortable for a busy woman moving from work in the factory, or on the land, back home to her family.

The turban also reflected a woman's working lifestyle. A scarf tied round the head kept hair away from dangerous machinery or hid unforgiving untidiness when there was little time to spend on grooming. Presentation was important for everyone, forming part of a patriotic lifestyle that helped to maintain morale during the war years.

The 'siren suit', famously worn by Churchill, was another fashionable and useful wartime outfit we recognise today as the original jumpsuit. All-in-one, all-covering, warm and zip-fronted, it was easy to put on as the sirens sounded in the event of a midnight air-raid. The origin of its name, therefore, was directly linked to its use.

The 'kangaroo cloak' was used in similar situations and, again, its name is a giveaway as to why it was worn: the large pockets could hold, for example, knitting needles, books or small toys.

It would appear then, that 'simple' is perhaps an accurate description of the confined 1940s British fashion, an era without unlimited pleats, pockets, frills and turn-ups. But women always found ways to add a touch of glamour and individuality into their wardrobes. The lack of silk and nylon stockings meant there was no alternative but to be inventive with makeup and even food supply.

As strange as it may sound, gravy browning was a good substitute for stockings. Smeared on the legs it would create the illusion of tanned skin, while lines drawn down the back of the legs with eyebrow pencil or eyeliner (to imitate stocking-seams) completed the look.

Some of these methods of appearing fashionable do not sound particularly appealing. Even so, where there was a will, there was a way, and women were enthusiastic about looking good.

'Girly' hairstyles were another way of achieving glamour and femininity in contrast to the boyish suits and sparing designs available. When hair wasn't up in a turban, the fashion was to wear it quite long, as length allowed experimentation and, usually, careful curls were the preferred style.

Accessories were regarded as unnecessary and thus subjected to a lot of customisation. A simple milk-top disk could be covered with raffia and any leftover scraps of material to create the ultimate fashion accessory and, as every woman would have you believe, a requirement for every outfit – the handbag.

So the war shed a new light on fashion and gave it perhaps more of a fundamental meaning than the ever-changing fashions of today. A smart appearance was no longer just for personal satisfaction, but in the midst of chaos, an act of defiance against the enemy.

Above all, it stood for patriotism and unity. Knitting balaclavas for troops, scrimping on design and re-using old clothes were all part of a nation pulling together, even in the smallest of ways, for the war effort. ■

'DOGGED DETERMINATION' HELPED WIN THE DAY

Dogs have worked tirelessly and given their lives in times of conflict for thousands of years, ever since the war dogs kept by the Egyptian Pharaohs. The Kennel Club, founded in 1873 and the governing body of the world of dogs, and British dog lovers have also traditionally played an integral part in the war effort, never more so than during World War II.

In the summer of 1940, the then Minister of Aircraft Production, Lord Beaverbrook, launched the Spitfire Fund, encouraging fundraising by organisations and companies that could be put towards production of the fighter plane. Each new Spitfire cost £5,000 and would bear a name relevant to the donor/s responsible.

Within weeks, the Kennel Club joined forces with two weekly canine newspapers, Our Dogs and Dog World, to launch the 'Dog Fighter Fund', an appeal to dog owners to help raise the money required to purchase a Spitfire by holding dog shows and donating the proceeds.

Donations from a single shilling upwards were publicly acknowledged across the canine publications and, within just three months the total collected stood at £6,290.7.5d, with the surplus funds put towards general Spitfire production.

The plane purchased with the money donated by dog lovers was built by Vickers Armstrong Supermarine and bore the name 'W3403 The Dogs Fighter'. It was given to the RAF at Brize Norton in June 1941 and entered active service the following month. In October of that year, the Kennel Club received a metal tablet from the Ministry, thanking them and the world of dogs, for their donation.

Several other appeals were also made to dog lovers during WWII. In April 1941, owners were asked to volunteer their dogs' services to the War Dog Training School at Aldershot and thousands obliged despite knowing they may never see their beloved pets again. Dogs were also donated for companionship to men serving at isolated Anti-Aircraft posts following an appeal to The Times newspaper.

Dogs continue to play a vitally important role in the armed forces today, having been actively involved in several recent conflicts. A prime example of this is Buster, an English Springer Spaniel army sniffer dog who has demonstrated his exceptional talents to uncover weapons.

Canine hero Buster

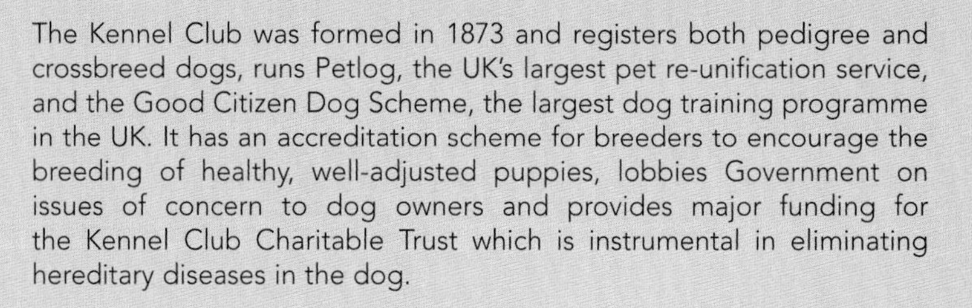

The Kennel Club was formed in 1873 and registers both pedigree and crossbreed dogs, runs Petlog, the UK's largest pet re-unification service, and the Good Citizen Dog Scheme, the largest dog training programme in the UK. It has an accreditation scheme for breeders to encourage the breeding of healthy, well-adjusted puppies, lobbies Government on issues of concern to dog owners and provides major funding for the Kennel Club Charitable Trust which is instrumental in eliminating hereditary diseases in the dog.

Sport took a back seat when Britain found itself under the threat of invasion. With the advent of conscription, many were called up, and many sports-grounds were expropriated for the war effort. By **Roger Linn**

Playing the game

The declaration of war in September 1939 was a knockout blow to all sport in Great Britain. It was as though the shock of what everybody had dreaded happening, actually coming to pass, simply stunned the bodies controlling the various popular sports.

There seem to have been no contingency plans for how to proceed in the event of hostilities and each individual sport's insularity from every other sport, as well as from government 'officialdom', meant that there was no collective decision-making.

Precipitate decisions made by these governing bodies, including football, racing and rugby, seemed to say, like Chicken Lickin', "The sky's falling down. The sky's falling down!" The FA, for instance, immediately ended contracts between players and clubs. Most professional football players received letters, such as the one pinned up in the Nottingham Forest changing room less than a week after the outbreak of war, as follows: "To the players – the Committee much regret that owing to present conditions they are unable to carry on the club in the normal way. Players are therefore at liberty to seek other employment and the Committee hope all will be successful in quickly obtaining work. When Football is permitted again – we shall immediately get in touch with you."

With such great events unfolding – the 1939-40 football league season opened on the day Germany invaded Poland – perhaps it is not surprising that there was no popular outcry at the demise of professional sport. The great majority are said to have accepted sport's disappearance with "the calm of people submerged in bewilderment".

As one observer eloquently put it, "For the first time, war broke the spell of sport, swept away steeple-chases,

A total of 266 Members of the Marylebone Cricket Club,
four of whom were holders of the Victoria Cross,
lost their lives during World War II
in the service of their country.

In recognition of the sacrifice which they made,
the Club is pleased to be associated with this
book and to wish the Ministry of Defence
every success with its publication.

Marylebone Cricket Club, Lord's Ground, London NW8 8QN

greyhounds and all-in wrestling, bowls and archery, fencing and tennis. The magic habit of recurring matches and goals and all the other elaborate weekly cycle brought out in the press, was broken."

Football teams initially faced a travel limit of 50 miles, the blackout and a maximum permitted gate of 8,000 spectators (later raised to 15,000 for clubs with a capacity of over 60,000). The FA and the League responded with regional football, which in one form or another, including a League (War) Cup, was to last throughout the war.

Team spirit

Effectively, this was a completely new set of circumstances and many of the rules had to be made up as the war progressed. Players in the armed forces, or on war work, were permitted to 'guest' for nearby clubs. So, for the spectator, until the sides ran out onto the pitch, there was no way of knowing who would be playing. Leslie Jones, the Welsh international, probably set the record when he managed to play for Fulham, West Ham and Southampton in the space of four days.

In the 1945 South Cup Final, Chelsea fielded eight guests, while Millwall selected four, and the clubs agreed to share the 12th man. Not infrequently, visiting sides would arrive without the required number of players, hoping to recruit the shortfall from the home team's reserves if they had any, or as a last resort, they would ask for volunteers from the crowd. This stratagem produced some interesting matches.

For example, one Christmas morning, Brighton travelled to Norwich, more in hope than expectation, as they only had five players. In the event, Norwich provided a couple of reserves and some soldiers volunteered to play. Brighton lost 18-0, which, incredibly, included an own goal.

The quality of the football was generally regarded as being much more entertaining than in pre-war days, with more goals being scored and players – freed from 'dressing room' instructions – being allowed to show off their talents.

"We had to play in our khaki knickers"

Madeline King (87) became an ATS girl.

"When things were pretty bad in 1940, I went along to the Army Ordnance Depot at Chilwell, Nottinghamshire and was taken on as a lorry driver – even though I was in a cotton dress and didn't really know whether I'd be able to drive a lorry or not. I was 22 at the time. I ended up driving the things for three years.

"I'd played cricket at school, so one day the adjutant sent for me and said I was to organise a match against a local men's team. They were to play left-handed to even things up and everybody thought it would be good for morale. The men certainly did because there wasn't any proper cricket kit and we had to play in our khaki knickers. We won, but they still wanted a return match."

But, initially at least, the crowds stayed away and this in a society where sport was regarded as being more important to the population than politics or religion.

There was a reluctance to travel far from home and many of the usual spectators had been called up, or were engaged in war work that precluded them from Saturday afternoon football-going. Representative games were, however, the exception. The Home Office was very keen on them for morale purposes. They had no crowd limitations and many of them were played to raise money for the Red Cross.

The Army side was popular, always drawing large crowds because it sometimes consisted entirely of international-class footballers. As restrictions became easier, gates improved, particularly for international matches, with a massive 133,000 spectators turning up at Glasgow's Hampden Park for the Scotland versus England match in 1944.

Joining forces

As an amateur sport, Rugby Union was able to carry on very much as before the war, although, like football, the first reaction of the RFU authorities had been to immediately cancel all fixtures. Wartime rugby became very like club cricket, with the game being played solely for the amusement of the players.

In fact, an early and unofficial varsity match, played at Cambridge, was so enjoyed by all concerned that they agreed to hold a return match two months later. In an uncharacteristic bout of warmth, the Twickenham authorities agreed to allow Union players dispensation to play alongside their League counterparts in Service matches, although not at other times.

What the League players thought of this charitable gesture is not recorded, but times were hard for those professionals who still endeavoured to play for money, because their pay had been reduced to £1 a game with no bonuses – they called it 'tea-party football'.

Back on track

Many racecourses were commandeered for military purposes, but horseracing survived in spite of the difficulties, which included considerable opposition among some sections of the population, as well as at Westminster, where racing was regarded by Mr Shinwell and his Labour party colleagues as elitist and a waste of resources. 'Manny', however, was informed in Parliament that if the oats fed to racehorses were instead to be fed to poultry, the saving would be one egg per head of population, once in four years.

Newmarket became the epicentre of the racing industry, with a number of important races, like the Sussex Stakes, being transferred to the course. All the classic races were run in front of large and enthusiastic crowds.

Perfect pitch

Cricket at the professional county-level was largely abandoned for the duration, as ground after ground was taken over for the war effort and transport around the country became impossible. Although the cricket authorities had some eight months after the start of the war in which to devise a structure for the 1940 season, they failed to come up with a plan.

The feeling was for one-day games to be improvised. The language of the game, however, became the language of war. We would, "Hit the Germans for six... Play with a straight bat" and "Prepare ourselves for a long innings".

"Pressure is a Messerschmitt up your arse, mate – not playing cricket!"

Of course, the villages continued to play against each other, just as they had in the last war – and for 100 years before that. In that long summer of 1940 (when the Battle of Britain was fought), the games in the south of England were played out under the white skein of contrails, which showed where the aerial battle was being fought high above them.

Cricket, which had started the war so unpromisingly soon gathered pace and, like football, began to offer an always-enthusiastic public a wide variety of representative fixtures, from local efforts like the London Fire Service versus the Met Police, to the rather more rarefied A.E.R. Gilligan's XI versus the RAF and the Empire XI versus the Combined Services.

Rich fare was to be found in these fixtures and the protagonists' names read like a roll call of cricket's greatest heroes: Bedser, Constantine, Hassett, Edrich, Compton and the iconic, multi-talented Australian, Keith Miller. Miller was a pilot in the RAAF when he was not playing cricket and when asked if he felt under pressure when walking out to bat at Lords, he is said to have replied: "Pressure is a Messerschmitt up your arse, mate – not playing cricket!" ■

Sources include:

The Mass-Observation Archive at Sussex University
Soccer At War by Jack Rollin
League Football by Simon Inglis
The Lost Seasons by Eric Midwinter
Graham Snelling, curator,
The National Horseracing Museum

Laurence Olivier and Renée Asherson in the 1945 film *Henry V*

A night at the pictures

Robin Cross explores the dual role that cinema played in wartime Britain – unifying the country and providing much-needed escapism from reality

In 1939, cinema was the world's most powerful medium of popular entertainment – the movies touched everybody's lives. In the six years that followed they became not only powerful instruments of national propaganda, but also an important medium of escapist entertainment and a relief from the hardships of war.

When war broke out in September 1939, the outlook for the British film industry was bleak. For two weeks the nation's cinemas were closed, a measure prompted by fear of massive casualties in a series of cataclysmic air raids. Simultaneously, a large amount of studio space was requisitioned for use in the so-called 'shadow factory' programme (see page 141 for further information on shadow factories) and for storage.

In the following months the film industry, like the nation itself, endured a kind of 'phoney war' before finding its feet and a sense of purpose. The mood was captured in Alexander Korda's *The Lion Has Wings*, the first British feature film of the war. An uneasy combination of drama and documentary, shot in less than two weeks during 1939, *The Lion Has Wings* featured Merle Oberon and Ralph Richardson as a 'typical English couple' telling each other, "We must fight for the things we believe in – truth and beauty, and kindness."

Although it now seems like a curious period piece, *The Lion Has Wings* did hint at a theme that was to become a staple of many British films of the conflict: the difference between Nazi Germany and Britain at war, the former fearsomely jackbooted and harshly robotic, the latter a combination of mildness and quirky good nature. At one point *The Lion Has Wings* cuts between Hitler in a paroxysm of demagogy at Nuremberg and the shy King George VI singing *Under the Spreading Chestnut Tree* at a Boy Scout jamboree.

The celebration of the cult genteel British 'amateur' pitted against blinkered and brutal Nazi thugs was a popular theme of the early war years. In films like *Night Train to Munich* (1940), Basil Radford and Naunton

Below: Ralph Richardson in *The Lion Has Wings*

Wayne reprised their roles from *The Lady Vanishes* (1938) as the bumbling, cricket-obsessed Charters and Caldicott, blindfolding a trussed-up Gestapo man with a convenient copy of *Mein Kampf*.

Pimpernel Smith (1941), starred Leslie Howard as a quizzical 1930s version of the Scarlet Pimpernel (a role Howard played in 1934), running an escape line for writers and scientists threatened with imprisonment by the Nazis.

The 'phoney war' was followed by a fight for national survival, which saw the Dunkirk evacuation (June 1940), the Battle of Britain (July-October 1940) and the Blitz on Britain's industrial cities and ports, the last running into the spring of 1941.

Simultaneously, British film-makers began to address the major themes of the conflict with a growing confidence. Britain was now mobilised to fight a People's War, and this was to be celebrated not in the pasteboard heroics of drawling, upper-class matinée idols but in the lives of ordinary soldiers and civilians.

Documentaries and propaganda

Critical in marking this sea change was the influence of the realist school of documentary film-making, fostered in the 1930s at the GPO Film Unit by John Grierson. The result was a steady stream of superb wartime documentaries and propaganda films, among them Harry Watt's *Target For Tonight* (1941), which followed a Bomber Command raid on Germany; Humphrey Jennings' *Fires Were Started* (1943), a moving exercise in what would now be called drama-documentary about a fire station at the height of the Blitz; and *Western Approaches* (1944), Pat Jackson's Technicolor account of the Battle of the Atlantic.

The wartime documentary played a vital role in cementing national solidarity, from modest Ministry of Information films on the vital but irksome rigours of wartime rationing, to movingly understated accounts of key Allied military campaigns like *Desert Victory* (1944) and *The True Glory* (1945), the latter produced in collaboration with US film-makers. Documentaries like these placed the lives of other ranks and the factory workforce centre-stage and, in turn, had a significant impact on feature films.

For example, in the unlikely hands of Noël Coward, 1942's *In Which We Serve* (which he co-directed with David Lean) told the story of a British warship, HMS *Torrin*, through the memories of her crew (the film was based on the true story of Lord Louis Mountbatten's destroyer, HMS *Kelly*); *Nine Men* (1943), directed by Harry

follow the election of a socialist government in the summer of 1945. A similar mood runs through Humphrey Jennings' elegiac documentary *A Diary for Timothy* (1945).

The mid-war years saw public interest in war subjects rise to a peak and then fall away. In January 1944, a Bristol woman wrote to her local newspaper, "I've just seen the Bette Davis film, *Now Voyager*, and what enjoyment and what relief – no war!" In addition to Hollywood melodramas and musicals, she could enjoy home-grown escapism in the form of the bravura cycle of costume dramas launched by Gainsborough Studio's *The Man in Grey* (1943) or musicals like Ealing's *Champagne Charlie* (1944), a lovingly-created evocation of Victorian popular entertainment.

Perhaps lost on wartime audiences were the more complex, multi-layered explorations of national narrative undertaken by the writer-director team of Michael Powell and Emeric Pressburger in *The Life and Death of Colonel Blimp* (1943) and *A Canterbury Tale* (1944).

More to contemporary taste was Laurence Olivier's *Henry V* (1945), whose sweeping battle scenes recalled Sergei Eisenstein's Alexander Nevsky. *Henry V*'s soaring box-office returns in the United States encouraged Britain's film financiers and makers to believe that in the post-war world they could take on the dominant Hollywood studios in their own market.

By 1945 it seemed that British cinema had come of age. Audiences were at an all-time high, climbing in 1946 to 1,356 million admissions, despite the fact that nearly 250 cinemas had been closed by bomb damage. The British film industry had emerged from the war in a mood of high optimism. ■

Watt, followed a group of Desert Rats surrounded by the enemy; Charles Frend's *San Demetrio, London* (1943) recounted the heroics of merchant seamen who sail a badly damaged tanker back to the Clyde; *Millions Like Us* (1943), directed by Frank Launder and Sidney Gilliat, tracked the lives of a group of 'mobile women' in a wartime armaments factory; Carol Reed's *The Way Ahead* (1944), was the British Army's equivalent of *In Which We Serve*, a microcosm of the nation that focused on the progress of a platoon of recruits, led by Territorial officer David Niven, from training to the battlefields of North Africa. Anthony Asquith's *The Way to the Stars* (1945) performed the same function for the men of RAF Bomber Command.

Social and political change

These films were made after the threat of German invasion had passed and while the British people, however apprehensively, were anticipating the end of the war and the social and political changes that would accompany the hard-won peace. Implicit in another Launder and Gilliat film, *Waterloo Road* (1944), a tentative early exercise on social realism, was the new social and political landscape, shaped by the People's War, which would

A DEBT OF GRATITUDE NEVER FORGOTTEN

TNT Express Services is proud to salute the courage of those who fought to maintain the liberty and freedom that the British people have enjoyed for the last 60 years. Their bravery and fortitude must never be forgotten and TNT is privileged to be playing its part in preserving the memory of their selfless actions, by safeguarding the military records of thousands upon thousands of servicemen and women.

A view on the past – Military service records are held at the TNT Archive Centre at Swadlincote in South Derbyshire

The service records are among more than 13 million documents that are entrusted to the keeping of TNT Archive Services – TNT's specialist records management division – under a 25-year agreement with the Ministry of Defence.

Dedicated

A prime example of a successful Private Finance Initiative (PFI) and Public Private Sector Partnership (PPP) project in action, the contract saw the construction by TNT of an £11 million, high security, showpiece archive centre, in South Derbyshire, to ensure the records are indexed, stored and maintained in peak condition.

Authorised officials select files and within hours the documents are delivered via TNT's extensive express delivery network and a fleet of dedicated vehicles from the company's instant-response same day service.

The Ministry of Defence contract is the latest in a succession of public/private sector agreements between TNT and the Government, stretching back many years.

The flagship 'Cross Government Courier Contract' – an agreement between TNT Managed Services and the Department of Work and Pensions and HM Revenue and Customs – sees the company collect, sort and deliver in excess of 100,000 items of mail, print and stationery every night for some 2,800 locations across the UK and Northern Ireland.

Integrity

TNT Managed Services – which specialises in providing office services and mailroom management solutions – has also developed an excellent working relationship with HM Revenue and Customs during a seven-year partnership.

On the record – handheld scanners help pinpoint Ministry of Defence documents safeguarded by TNT Archive Service

Integrity, honesty and reliability have been the key qualities in the agreement under which TNT transport a multitude of goods to storage locations across the UK.

Innovation

For more than a quarter of a century, TNT Express Services UK and Ireland has been serving the time-sensitive express delivery needs of government and industry alike. The first company in the UK to launch nationwide, next day and same day deliveries, TNT has established an enviable reputation for quality, innovation and customer service.

The 60 years since the end of the Second World War have been especially significant for TNT. Our founder, Ken Thomas, started the company in Australia in the immediate aftermath of the conflict in 1946, buying two trucks – Samson and Delilah – to provide an express delivery service to the first ever customers Down Under.

The rest, as they say, is history.

Tuned in

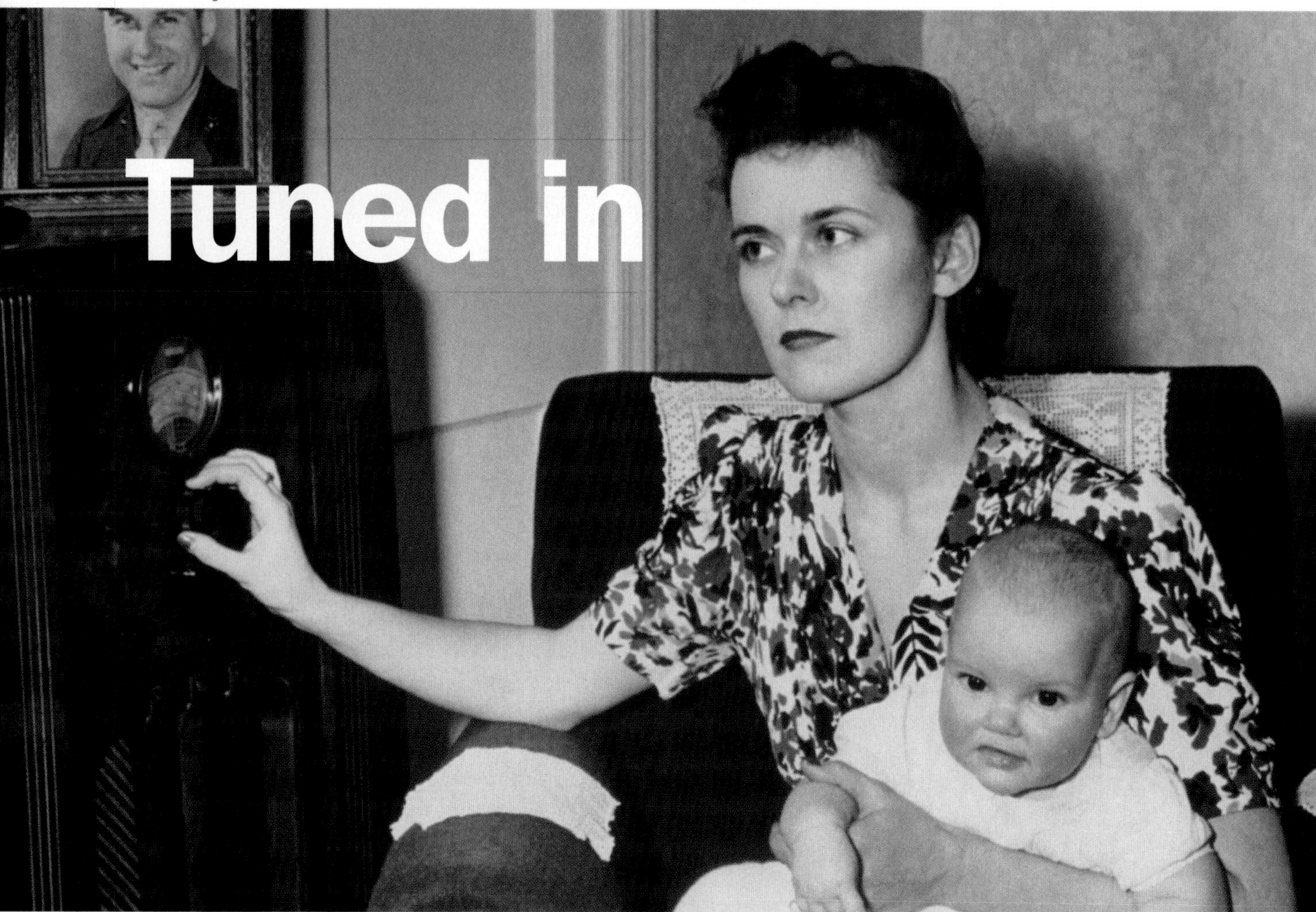

Radio was an essential form of communication, which attracted millions of listeners and also kept the troops entertained. By **Howard Gossington**

Nowadays, 'the box' in the corner of the room that keeps us entertained is either the TV, connected to the DVD, or a PC/games console. In 1945, however, it was the radio, or to give it its more usual name – the wireless.

As the war progressed, millions tuned in to hear the latest news, a message from Churchill or one of the many popular variety shows. In the various theatres of war, it kept the troops both informed and entertained.

In 1939, an incipient BBC broadcast its radio output on both a national network and seven regional services. When Hitler marched into Poland on Friday September 1, the BBC merged its radio output into a single 'Home Service', and suspended television broadcasts altogether, for fear the transmitters might be used by the enemy.

But the content of the BBC's radio output at the outbreak of war was hardly something to write home about, argues Tom Hickman, author of a history of the BBC during the war: "They played records, drove people mad with a chap called Sandy MacPherson at the organ – he was originally the organist at The Empire Cinema, Leicester Square – and let a lot of bumptious officials on the air." News output was limited to official communiqués, heavily censored by the military and the newly created Ministry of Information, to whom the BBC was now accountable.

The British Expeditionary Force (BEF) in Northern France was hardly excited by this listening fare, and

PRICE TWOPENCE

PROGRAMMES FOR February 18—24

RADIO TIMES

JOURNAL OF THE BRITISH BROADCASTING CORPORATION

(INCORPORATING WORLD-RADIO)

FOR THE FORCES

The twelve-hour daily programmes start this week

The service of special programmes intended for men of the Navy, Army, and Air Force is being extended to twelve hours daily, from 11 a.m. to 11 p.m. Full details of all programmes are now given in the RADIO TIMES side by side with details of the Home Service programmes. Information about the new service will be found on page 3.

RADIO TIMES SUPPLEMENTARY ISSUE, September 4, 1939, Vol. 64, No. 831A

Price TWOPENCE

RADIO TIMES

JOURNAL OF THE BRITISH BROADCASTING CORPORATION

(INCORPORATING WORLD-RADIO)

REVISED PROGRAMMES for Sept. 4-10

BROADCASTING CARRIES ON

PRICE TWOPENCE

PROGRAMMES FOR February 9—15

RADIO TIMES

JOURNAL OF THE BRITISH BROADCASTING CORPORATION

(INCORPORATING WORLD-RADIO)

THIS WEEK

BBC Theatre Orchestra

'A Play is Born'

'Speak of the Devil'

Billy Milton

Scott and Whaley

The Planets

Edmund Burke

Sir Donald Tovey

'CHILDREN CALLING HOME'

instead tuned their radios to the French commercial stations. So, the BBC canvassed the views of the troops and on January 7 1940 launched the Forces Programme network. "It was unbelievably popular," says Hickman. "It may sound sentimental now, but it was a major factor in reminding the men that dear old Blighty was still there and was what they were fighting for."

Now the troops could get their fill of light music and dance bands, concert parties, record requests, sports commentaries, and even French lessons.

The Forces Programme also became the station of choice for much of the civilian population; many items went out on both networks. "The 9pm news bulletin was the highpoint of the listening day," explains Terry Charman, a historian at the Imperial War Museum. "Everybody sat around the radio and listened to that. Then after the news on a Sunday, you had a five-minute slot, *Postscript*. The playwright J B Priestley was the most famous broadcaster, but people like the film star Leslie Howard, and even George Formby, gave postscripts." It was also the slot Churchill used to stiffen the nation's resolve with many of his famous speeches.

Undoubtedly, though, it was variety that spawned some of the nation's favourite radio stars. "The most popular show of the war was *ITMA – It's That Man Again!* – starring Tommy Handley," says Hickman. "Newspapers said that if Germany was going to invade it should do so at half-past eight on a Thursday evening – everyone in Britain, including the King, was listening to *ITMA*."

Popular radio entertainer Tommy Handley (right) at the microphone with Clarence Wright during a wartime BBC variety show

It was variety that spawned some of the nation's favourite radio stars

Other popular variety shows included *Hi Gang!* (featuring Churchill's son-in-law, Vic Oliver), *Happidrome* (set in a mythical theatre) and *Band Waggon* with Arthur Askey and Richard Murdoch. The radio also came, quite literally, to the people with the dance bands of *Music While You Work* visiting different factories every week.

Workers' Playtime featured comedy acts recorded on location during the lunch break. Vera Lynn was

officially crowned 'Forces' Sweetheart', topping a popularity poll among the BEF, thanks to her show, *Sincerely Yours*.

Even a group of academics gained an unlikely place in the nation's heart, in a show called *The Brains Trust*. "Initially, it was designed for people in the forces to send in letters," Charman explains. "The questions were like: 'Is there a God?' 'Where do flies go in the winter?' It started broadcasting in January 1941 and soon had a terrific audience, and the permanent panellists became personalities in their own right."

On the home front, programmes offering practical advice for making rations go further (*The Kitchen Front*), caring for allotments (*Backs to the Land*), and keeping fit and healthy (*Up in the Morning Early*) attracted millions of listeners.

On the cultural side, the BBC churned out some 400 radio plays a year. In 1943, it began one of the most popular drama series of the war, *Appointment with Fear*.

The BBC massively increased its international coverage, so that by the end of the war it transmitted in no fewer than 45 languages, compared with just seven at the start. Meanwhile, the influx of American troops into the British Isles meant the Forces Programme now had to cater for a new audience. On February 27 1944, it became the General Forces Programme, retaining old favourites and bringing in programmes new to the British public, such as a review of the British press.

On the eve of D-Day (June 6 1944), the BBC launched a programme that would change the face of news reporting forever. *War Report* carried the first account of the Normandy landings by correspondents in the field. "There had never been anything like it," says Hickman, "and the nation was glued to its sets. Until 1944 only brief war dispatches had been carried in the news. Now the war had its own half-hour programme." *War Report* ran virtually uninterrupted every night until the end of the war.

When VE Day (May 8 1945) finally came, the BBC broadcast 10 days of celebration programmes, including a nightly retrospective, *Their Finest Hour*, and victory versions of all the variety favourites. The General Forces programmes ended, and on July 29 1945, the Light Programme began, running alongside the Home Service and the re-instated regional services. June 1946 saw the re-introduction of television, resuming with the same Mickey Mouse cartoon that had been so rudely interrupted six years earlier.

By the end of the war, the number of radio licences had risen to 11 million and might have gone higher but for the lack of radio sets. "The BBC had become an indispensable part of British national life," says Hickman. "Outside Britain the scale and authority of its news was unrivalled. In the occupied countries of Europe the BBC was a lifeline – people risked execution to own radio sets. Where 'Auntie Beeb' had once been a derogatory term, now it was one of affection." ■

Manchester Commemorates and Celebrates

The people of Manchester have commemorated and celebrated the 60th Anniversary of the end of the Second World War to show respect and honour to a generation who lived so bravely through turbulent times.

On May 8 2005 - sixty years exactly since Victory in Europe - the city unveiled a new memorial to the civilians who died in Manchester as a result of enemy action. During Second World War bombing raids, more than 700 Manchester people were killed and 2,300 injured. A total of 50,000 homes were hit and 30 acres of buildings in the city centre were damaged, including many of the most historic.

The names of loved ones who died during those bombings are now etched on the trunk of a 12-metre high metallic tree of remembrance. The steel, copper and bronze structure stands as a spiritual focus in Piccadilly Gardens providing a place for quiet contemplation and memory. Representatives from all faith groups paid tribute during its poignant unveiling, performed by the Lord Mayor of Manchester Councillor Tom O'Callaghan.

A number of traditional war memorials across the city are also being refurbished as a mark of respect and a wide range of outdoor celebrations have been held in the streets of Manchester to invoke the spirit of relief felt by revellers during the summer of 1945. Councillor Val Stevens, deputy leader of Manchester City Council, said: "We are delighted that people are taking this opportunity to remember and to celebrate this historic event. It is a time to honour the courage of all the ordinary Manchester men, women and children forced to live through extraordinary times."

Almost 180 community events took place across Manchester on Sunday May 8, made possible by grants of up to £500 each, awarded by the City Council. Families ate and drank at street parties; pensioners remembered times gone by and treasured mementoes such as gas masks and recipes were shown off to younger generations. In the city's main squares - where in 1945 crowds listened to tannoys transmitting Prime Minister Winston Churchill - a festival of music, dancing and entertainment re-created the Victory atmosphere. Crowds of visitors turned up in wartime costumes to be transported back to the era of Glen Miller, Vera Lynn, Flanagan and Allen, George Formby, Gracie Fields, the Andrews' Sisters and more.

To eat and drink, there were non-rationed treats, such as cream teas, hearty pies, Vimto and dandelion and burdock on party benches and chairs in Albert Square, surrounded by the historic jeeps and army vehicles. In the evening there was a big screen television linking swing bands in Manchester to London's Trafalgar Square where big name stars and celebrities called upon the audience to remember the generation that sacrificed so much. The city's libraries held exhibitions of wartime experiences, including a chronicle of the war from the Soviet perspective. Dozens of photographs portraying the 900-day siege of Leningrad - now known as St Petersburg and Manchester's friendship city - were on display in Central Library.

Manchester is also proud to support events on July 10 2005 - The National Commemoration of the 60th Anniversary of the End of World War II. And on Sunday August 14, the city will commemorate the anniversary of the end of the war in Japan and to ensure future generations never forget the times and lessons of this epic period in history, Manchester has commissioned a History Project, recording people's experiences of those turbulent times. Residents have been interviewed about living in the city, or serving in other parts of the world during the Second World War. An audio CD of memories will be published later this year covering the tapestry of wartime experiences including weddings, schooldays, munitions, the Manchester blitz and the role of women.

Said Councillor Stevens: "The Second World War played a major role in shaping Manchester's future, both physically and through its effect on all those who lived and served through those difficult years. We respect that brave generation for facing tremendous challenges, and it is essential that we remember and honour them in years to come. Manchester is delighted to play a leading role in commemorating and celebrating this 60th anniversary of the end of the Second World War.

An inspired blend of hops, maize, yeast, barley malt, rice and determination.

Raising a glass to the future

The pub remained a mainstay of the community, where information could be shared and people came together to support one another. A place to enjoy rather than to feel sorrow. By **Roger Linn**

South London on a Saturday night in 1943. The blackout regulations make it difficult to locate the pub as no light or any other sign of gaiety spills out onto the pavement. Both the Public and the Saloon bars are crowded with an exotic mixture of people and uniforms. The Public bar, with its benches, dartboard and hard chairs, sells beer at a penny a pint less than the Saloon and is populated by the 'lower' classes and the elderly.

In the Saloon, there are carpets on the floor, tables, some easy chairs and even pictures on the walls. Nearly everybody is smoking – Goldflake, Players, Senior Service and Craven 'A' in the Saloon and, more modestly, Players Weights and Woodbine in the Public.

A resolute woman pianist is gamely playing hits from a new Hollywood musical, *For Me and My Gal*, accompanied by a young airman who has brought a piano accordion to the pub. Later, the songs become old favourites like *Tipperary*, *If You Were The Only Girl In The World* and *Goodbye Dolly Gray*.

> People are here to forget and to sing – just for a while

The landlord, like many, believes that a good bookie is an asset to a pub and his 'runner' is going round settling up for today's racing. As well as the men in reserved occupations, there are members of all the armed forces in here, including colonial troops from all over the world. There are several Canadians and the Yanks, of course, are surrounded by girls and buying rounds as though the war is over.

The men are drinking pints of bitter or mild and bitter. Some of the girls are also drinking beer, partly to make the point that if they can do a man's work, then they can drink a man's brew.

People are here to ease the pain of long partings; or, in some cases, of loss; to seek communal laughter when solitary sadness might be the only other option. To forget and to sing – just for a while.

A time of adjustment

Following the outbreak of war in 1939, the pub-going community changed dramatically. In the months immediately after the declaration of war, attendance slumped by nearly 40 per cent, as people anxiously and

Women had all the work they wanted, which meant money in their pockets

somewhat fearfully tried to adjust to the new circumstances. Indeed, for a short time in 1940, there was a vogue for 'bottle parties', with Express Wine Services offering a nightly delivery service to meet demand.

However, it wasn't long before pub-attendance recovered to pre-war numbers, albeit the make-up of the regulars had changed. In urban and suburban areas, women formed some 25 per cent of the pub's clientele, whereas before the war, unaccompanied females were quite rare.

The reasons for this influx aren't hard to find: young women could have all the work they wanted and that meant money in their pockets and nothing to spend it on; the young chaps were in the services, so the girls went out on their own for a bit of a laugh.

New moral standards

Now it's 1943, and there are shop-girls, nurses, girls from the buses and servicewomen, many of whom are away from home for the first time. And it is not only the girls who are experimenting with this newfound freedom. One or two of the young men look a bit too young to be served in here as well, but 16-year-olds can now earn a man's wages labouring, and they like to splash it about a bit. Some of them even go to the pictures twice a week.

A lot of the older male members of the population aren't very keen on the idea of all these young people enjoying themselves and there is much talk about declining moral standards but, by and large, the changes are seen as inevitable. The general feeling is best expressed by one of the bar staff, as he pulls another pint of warm mild for a pre-war regular who's not so happy about things. "It makes the pub nice and lively, so long as they don't get blind drunk. Them ATS girls can only do a couple of large scotches before they're trying to dance *Knees-up Mother Brown* on the tables."

It is a lot quieter during the week of course – a bit like it was in the Blitz in the winter of 1940-41 when most people went home early. Mostly, it is just locals dropping in for a pint and a bit of company while they listen to the pub's wireless. They always have it on for the news, of course, and there's usually something to cheer you up, like *ITMA* or Max Millar.

This is a different Britain from the last war, when Lloyd George famously remarked, "We are fighting Germany, Austria and Drink and, as far as I can see, the greatest of these deadly foes is Drink." Temperance societies are less powerful now than they were then and there doesn't seem to be the same concern that workers in vital industries, like munitions, will spend all their pay on drink to the detriment of their work.

Whereas in the last war, the government influenced the strength of the beer in public houses and even brought in laws to stop 'treating' in pubs. The current government has recognised the pub for the cultural institution it is and for its contribution to public morale and togetherness.

People are now spending more of their time in pubs than in any other building away from their homes or workplaces. And pubs are taking more money than cinemas, dancehalls and all other social gatherings combined.

It will be interesting to see if these changes to pub life will be reflected in the rest of society when the war is over, and whether or not young people and women will continue to make up a significant proportion of pub goers. Many can't see the world going back to the way it was. As Judy Garland sings in *For Me and My Gal*, "How ya gonna keep 'em down on the farm after they've seen Paree?" ■

PRAGUE STOCK EXCHANGE

LIVING IN THE CENTRE OF EUROPE, WE KNOW WELL THE TRAGEDY OF WARFARE. INDEED, MOST OF THE CONFLICTS IN MODERN EUROPEAN HISTORY HAVE SCARRED OUR COUNTRY. NONE OF THEM, HOWEVER, HAS RESULTED IN SUCH LOSS OR SUFFERING AS WORLD WAR II.

THEREFORE, WE DOUBLY APPRECIATE THE COURAGE AND SACRIFICE OF EVERY MAN AND WOMAN FROM THE ALLIED NATIONS WHO OFFERED THEIR BRAVERY AND THEIR LIVES TO BRING FREEDOM AND PEACE TO EUROPE.

ON THIS 60TH ANNIVERSARY WE THANK YOU, THE VETERANS, FOR ALL THAT YOU GAVE

PETR KOBLIC
Chairman
Prague Stock Exchange

Keeping up morale

Despite daily attacks by the Luftwaffe, Britain displayed a brave face to the world. **Howard Gossington** looks at the way in which the media helped to keep up morale and convey the message that Britain's spirit was far from broken

Newspapers, cinemas and, especially, the radio relayed news of the war to the British public like never before. As the entire country pulled together in the single cause of defeating Hitler, so it became vital that no word or image in the vast output of printed stories, newsreels or wireless bulletins said anything that could undermine that effort.

The message to the world had to be that despite the daily onslaught from the Luftwaffe, life in Britain carried on inexorably towards victory.

The government, through its newly created Ministry of Information, insisted that any news item fulfilled two criteria. "The first was 'not to give aid, comfort or information to the enemy'," explains Terry Charman, historian at the Imperial War Museum. "So, in a photograph of Churchill inspecting British troops just before D-Day, the men's flashes of which unit they served would have been scrubbed out by the censor."

Other off-limits details included troop numbers or geographic locations, which would have been removed by the military before the official communiqués were issued.

The whereabouts of the Cabinet and royal family were also no-go items, as were weather forecasts, for fear that reports of clear skies or fog would influence Luftwaffe bombing decisions.

Censorship also applied to letters home from the front, with any offending words scored out by the military. That's not to say the troops didn't try and cram in a bit of colour, as Charman points out, "Often, you see things like: 'I can't tell you where I am, but it's where Annie and Ted went on their honeymoon!'"

Weekly newsreels became an important means of watching the war

The second censorship rule, and more difficult to interpret, was that 'nothing be said that could diminish the nation's morale'. "At the beginning of the war, everything was talked about in terms of protecting morale," says Dr Sian Nicholas, lecturer in history at the University of Wales, Aberystwyth. "In the early part of the war, there was a real fear of releasing any bad news."

Examples abound where events were either not reported, or news was delayed to limit the negative impact. "When France asked for an armistice on June 17 1940, the transport ship, the *Lancastria*, was bombed outside of Saint-Nazaire," Charman explains. "Thousands of people were killed or injured. Churchill directly intervened to suppress the story, saying there had been enough depressing news that day."

Often the strategy was to portray events in their most positive light. For example, news of the Dunkirk evacuations in 1940, after the advancing Germans drove the British Expeditionary Force back to the French coast, became a story of triumph. Churchill described it as a "miracle".

"Dunkirk was one occasion where journalists felt they couldn't tell the whole story," says Dr Nicholas. "It's a news story spun out of all recognition, but you can exactly see why. People needed hope, so it was an absolutely instinctive reaction by the reporters to pick out the good news."

Boosting morale

After the Dieppe raid of August 1942, when the Allied Forces' attempted landing ended in disaster, some journalists like the BBC's Frank Gillard regretted that more of the truth hadn't been told. As Charman describes: "The reason why we went and the lack of success are very fudged in the press reports. They tend to dwell on individual exploits rather than the failure of the whole thing."

Reporting the Blitzing of British cities presented the news media with another dilemma. "During the Swansea Blitz, the BBC sent back some very upbeat dispatches about how well everyone's doing," confirms Dr Nicholas. "A lot of people in Swansea complained, saying actually they were in a miserable situation. When York was Blitzed, the BBC reported that York Minster hadn't been destroyed – people were worried that the Luftwaffe would come back to finish the job. On the other hand, you ran the risk that if you didn't report a Blitz, people would say: 'Well, you reported Plymouth – why not us?'"

As well as limiting the impact of bad news, the media made the most of military successes. Perhaps the most famous example was the Dambusters' Raid of May 1943, when the Lancaster bombers dropped their bouncing bombs to destroy the Ruhr Dams. "The Dambusters' Raid was portrayed as a great success," explains Charman. "Guy Gibson was given the Victoria Cross, which he richly deserved, but as well as a strategic exercise, it was a morale-boosting one. It did do damage, but the way it was presented in the newspapers the next day, it was almost 'well, that's the Ruhr knocked out'."

News on film

1940s Britain was very much a nation of cinemagoers, and the weekly newsreels became an important means of watching the war. These would usually begin with news on the fighting, although the cameras could only venture where the military, and the constraints of their cumbersome equipment, allowed. Visits by royalty or Churchill occupied much footage. "Then there was a showbiz type of feature," says Charman. "Gracie Fields, Vera Lynn or George Formby entertaining the troops. I think as the war went on, a lot of people found that escapism was the most important thing."

In 1943, the BBC changed the nature of media war-coverage by setting up its own war-reporting unit, comprising, for the first time, a dedicated news-gathering department.

Richard Dimbleby (centre) edits a recorded news item for the BBC

As well as limiting the impact of bad news, the media made the most of military successes

Later that year, the BBC issued its correspondents with a portable wind-up recorder known as the 'midget', allowing them to record despatches in the field and send the discs back for broadcasting. "This is the first time the BBC really sets about using proper roving war-reporters," says Dr Nicholas. "It was a wonderfully eclectic department. You had Richard Dimbleby, who was the BBC's first news observer before the war, but they also roped-in sports reporters like Stuart Hibbert, and people who'd been doing the royal parades; correspondents who could talk about what they were seeing."

This style of reportage proved incredibly popular, even if early examples were somewhat controversial. During the Battle of Britain (July-October 1940), war reporter Charles Gardner commentated on a dogfight over the Straits of Dover. "He got incredibly excited, but more people liked it than didn't, and it just brought something really fresh and novel," Dr Nicholas explains. "Suddenly you got the idea that you could use eye-witness reporting in a way that brought the war into the home in a very positive way, and made people feel engaged in the war."

When D-Day (June 6 1944) finally came, the BBC launched *War Report*, a nightly half-hour programme of war news. People at home listened as Chester Wilmot reported from the inside of a glider with airborne troops heading for France; Michael Standing described the scene off the Normandy coast as the landings approached and General Montgomery bade the troops, "Good luck and good hunting on the mainland of Europe". "It's how millions followed the war until the end," confirms Dr Nicholas. "I think it really transformed the way people experienced war at home, linking home fronts and battle fronts."

Undoubtedly, as the war progressed, the government became far more trusting of journalists not to make 'careless talk', recognising that everyone was fighting the same cause. "Certainly, the official censors get to recognise they don't need to be breathing down the media's neck all the time," Dr Nicholas explains. And even though paper-rationing limited broadsheets to just four pages of news, she argues that historians still refer to the war years as a "golden age for press reporting."

"News of the war portrayed a people united in their suffering," Charman concludes, "but with a very important message: 'Britain can take it.'" ■

Sonar and radar turned the tide of the Battle of the Atlantic

The UK managed to push forward the frontiers of science and technology

Work and travel

The industrial effort

Wars of national survival – total war – require that huge resources and capabilities be harnessed. For the United Kingdom, World War II was no exception as the whole nation pulled together as never before. By **Paul Beaver**

Britain did not start from scratch in 1939. The growing might of Nazi Germany, especially in aviation and armoured vehicle production, had been noted by the government of the day three years earlier.

Consequently, plans were made to create 'shadow factories' to be used should the existing industrial base be attacked from the air. The plans were carefully crafted with shadow factory locations chosen where there was already a pool of skilled craftsmen.

The Air Ministry was particularly busy in finding sites and selected Swindon, the mighty Wiltshire railway town and home of the Great Western Railway, with its pool of tradesmen, craftsmen and labourers. Swindon's South Marston airfield and factory complex was designated to shadow the Reading site of Phillips & Powis Aircraft, which made training aircraft that were vital to the war effort by bringing on pilots for Fighter Command and, later, Bomber Command. In the industrial West Midlands, luxury motorcars were irrelevant during World

Decoded
Bletchley Park 1945
GCHQ Cheltenham 2005
+60=
YEARS
Codebreakers' Hut at Bletchley Park.
GCHQ's new building at Cheltenham.
On VE day 1945, Bletchley Park codebreakers were still working on solving the Japanese ciphers. By the end of the war there were over 10,000 people, 11 "Colossi" (the world's first semi-programmable electronic computer) and 200 "Bombe" code breaking machines, all part of the world's first large-scale codebreaking organisation. The work of Bletchley Park helped shorten WW2 by up to two years and laid the foundations for today's GCHQ at Cheltenham.
Bletchley Park is now a heritage site run by a charitable Trust, with historic buildings, exhibitions and tours for visitors, special events, learning programmes and conference facilities.
BLETCHLEY PARK
National Codes Centre
Tel: 01908 640404
OPEN DAILY
www.bletchleypark.org.uk
Bletchley Park Trust, The Mansion, Bletchley, Milton Keynes MK3 6EB
1945. War ends.
the battle continues
Thanks to the code breakers at Bletchley Park, the Second World War ended sooner than it might. They were the silent heroes who helped bring the conflict to a favourable conclusion. But 60 years later, the fight for national security still goes on. Since the days of the famous enigma machine, the threat has changed. And GCHQ has changed with it. Although we're every bit as low profile, our methods are increasingly hi-tech. The legacy that Bletchley Park created is still saving lives, but our technology has evolved to keep us at the cutting edge. To safeguard Britain against international terrorists, drug barons and computer hackers, we gather and analyse vital intelligence using some of the world's most powerful IT systems. But like at Bletchley, it's our people who help make the difference. Comprising mathematicians, linguists and IT specialists - as well as a number of generalist support roles - we're a diverse team with many different skills. But together, we make GCHQ a formidable arm of British Intelligence. And you could be a part of it.
Visit www.gchq.gov.uk for more information on the organisation and career opportunities.

Business as usual

Despite the inevitable disruption caused by the war, businesses of all sizes played a vital part in the war effort. By **Andrew Maiden**

The onset of war disrupted numerous lives. Parents, sons, daughters all had their fair share of having to cope with the unexpected and unpredictable. Apart from the changes forced on ordinary people, there were various demands on British business, not only to support the war effort, but also to provide goods and services to the British people, from the scarce available resources. Keeping morale high was also a task for the business sector, via its drive, stability and visibility.

All over the country, British business successfully mobilised thousands of workers into useful war production. For example, Boots the Chemist may seem an unlikely company to help boost the war effort. Yet, John Boot himself was appointed Regional Commissioner for Civil Defence for the North Midlands, as well as remaining chairman of the company.

Meanwhile, Boots' manufacturing capacity was geared towards the war effort, producing, for instance, 1,339 tons of saccharine (equivalent to around 730,000 tons of sugar, a commodity which was strictly rationed). In addition, 50 million bottles of orange juice were packed for the Ministry of Food, and 1,500 tons of Chloramine were produced for water sterilisation in Europe, Africa and the Far East. The company also manufactured penicillin in the largest surface-culture plant in the country, designed and managed on behalf of the Ministry of Supply.

All this considerable activity was achieved while 7,000 employees were away on war duty. By war's end, 381

Cadbury's part in the war effort

As with many businesses, World War II had a profound effect on Cadbury and, in particular, its spiritual home in Bournville, Birmingham.

The outbreak of war in 1939 saw a host of factories in the industrial heartland of the West Midlands turned over to military production. Yet it was not just the metal-working companies, such as Lucas and BSA, who played their part. While many of its employees went into the armed services, Cadbury directors met in spring 1940 to form Bournville Utilities in conjunction with the government.

Two thousand workers, most of them women, were transferred to war work and, while a number of aircraft parts were produced in Bournville, it was the manufacture of gas masks for which Bournville Utilities was perhaps best known, with more than 5 million produced on site.

Change was not just restricted to manufacturing – the effects of war were all around Bournville. Sixteen-year-old Margaret Smith, she later recalled, left her work on gas masks to tend occasionally to the war-wounded, who were convalescing in a section of the canteen.

Seventeen-year-old Norman Sabin would keep an eye out for enemy aircraft as a roof spotter, among the camouflaged buildings: "As soon as the air raid siren went, we rushed to the look-out post ready with five rounds of ammunition – to shoot the enemy down." Norman never got to use his ammunition and the factory escaped damage, despite bombs falling nearby.

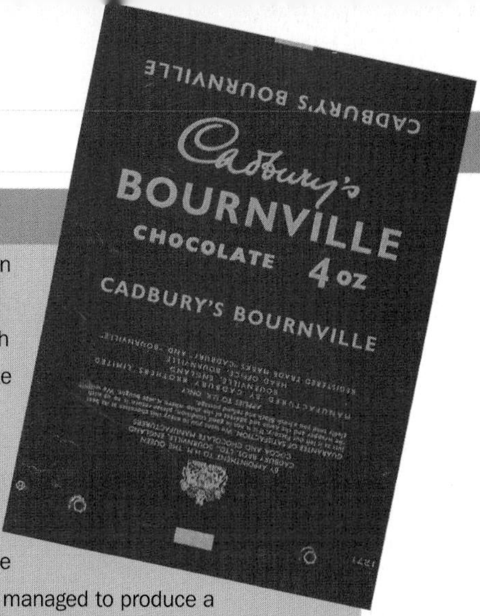

Cadbury played its part in other ways too, with its famous 'mercy vans', which braved air raids to distribute mugs of hot chocolate. This came at a time when the raw ingredients for chocolate, such as cocoa, milk and sugar, were difficult to obtain. Cadbury managed to produce a 'ration' chocolate which, as its name suggests, was rationed by the government to just 3oz per week per person. Despite this, Cadbury continued to advertise brands such as Dairy Milk at a time when they were not even on sale – the far-sighted directors knew they had to keep alive the memory of these favourites until a time when peace and prosperity returned once more.

The post-war years were difficult for Cadbury as shortages of supplies and labour, along with continued rationing, forced the firm to work around the problems. Ironically, the need to concentrate on fewer lines and a focus on how they could meet the needs of the post-war generation helped the business recover, as brands such as Dairy Milk became ever more popular. And, when rationing finally ended in 1953, Cadbury was a fit and lean business, able to renew its position as the leading UK confectionery company.

CADBURY'S BOURNVILLE
Cadbury's
BOURNVILLE
CHOCOLATE 4oz
CADBURY'S BOURNVILLE

Boots employees had been killed, either in battle or during air raids.

Some of the shops were also used as first aid posts, attended by qualified nurses. The chemist employed at the Boots store in Lambeth was awarded the George Cross for rescuing a wounded man from a blazing aeroplane loaded with bombs.

In 1942, the main factory of Vickers-Armstrong in Brooklands, Surrey was in full production. Each worker toiled for eight hours each shift. But the day after Winston Churchill's Dunkirk speech, the workers were inspired to call a meeting in the canteen where they all volunteered to work extra hours, without pay, to help the war effort. From then on, this became the norm. This extra effort and determination meant that the company was able to produce three Wellington bombers every 24 hours.

Small individual contributions combined to make a difference

It was at the company's hangar, W46, Byfleet, Surrey that the company worked on a top-secret project headed by Dr Barnes Wallis. In 1943, the Dambuster Raids, by the RAF's 617 Squadron, were carried out against the Moehne, Eder and Sorpe dams. It was only after the raids had been reported, that the workers became aware that they had been engaged in prototype tests of Wallis's Bouncing Bomb. From hard work and committed endeavour, small individual contributions combined to make a difference.

Thank you

from everyone at GNER

60th Anniversary of Victory in 1945

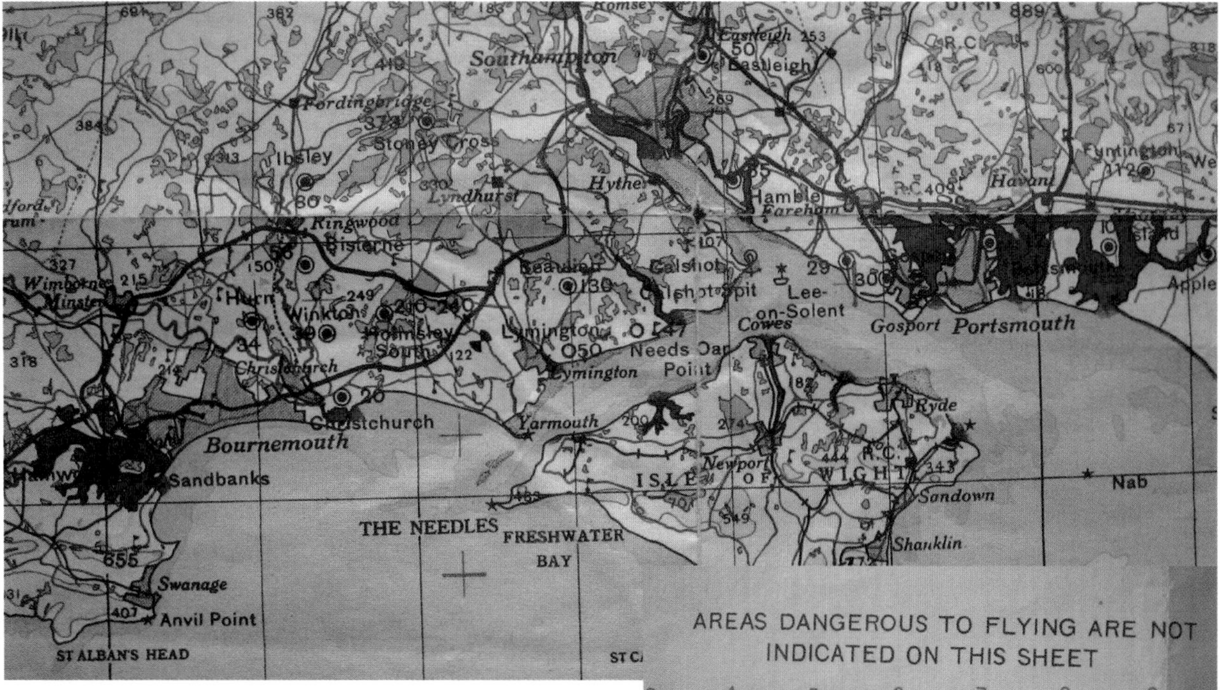

In 1943, workers at Fields Printers in Bradford were given the job of printing maps from artwork the size of a postage stamp. Fields were more used to printing cigarette packaging, but the maps had to be printed full-size on litho paper. Some of the printers recognised that the maps depicted part of France. However, once again, they were not to know until several months later that they had assisted RAF navigators during the D-Day invasion (June 6 1944).

Frank Gallard worked for a builder called Ackworth, who had teams of young lads and older men engaged in bomb-damage repairs, known as first aid repairs. When a bomb dropped in an area, they were sent to put up blackouts (black bitumen-felt) over the windows that had been blown out.

One particular time, in Edmonton, his group were called to repair damaged tiles on a roof. When it was time to finish for the day, Frank still had a couple of tiles in his hand, so he placed them against a chimney pot and made his way home. More raids followed. When he returned to the site, a bomb had fallen close to where he had been working. All the tiles were blown from the roof, yet the tiles he had left on the chimney-stack remained untouched.

Workers were given the job of printing maps from artwork the size of a stamp

The women who worked at Rolls-Royce in Derby were taught how to read micrometers for examining aeroplanes. During air raids, they huddled in the cellars. After a raid had passed, the women emerged singing songs that they had learnt from a gramophone kept in the cellars. Elsie Church recalls: "We knew our work was very important. We called the RAF 'the Boys in Blue'. That's why our work had to be accurate, because their lives depended on our being careful. We were all very proud. I was, and all my friends were. Well, it was our country that we were fighting for."

"We can all feel proud that every Briton played his or her part"

Many civilians who had not been called up proved themselves willing and determined to play their part in supporting the country during this difficult time. It wasn't just sheer determination, mettle, or acts of generosity and bravery that were shown by business leaders and their employees, there was something that was almost more important: innovation and ingenuity. Developments in medical efficiency, new aircraft designs and other breakthroughs helped to give the British war effort an edge over their enemies.

The individual efforts of British companies made an exceptional contribution to sustaining the British way of life. It wasn't until 20 years after the end of the war that the Confederation of British Industry (CBI) was formed. Britain's 'business voice' is a significant lobbying force to successive governments, ensuring that business is at the centre of their plans. Perhaps the war effort would have benefited from such an organisation?

"The sheer scale of the support that businesses provided towards the war effort is staggering," observes current CBI Director-General, Sir Digby Jones. "We can all feel proud that every Briton played his or her part. For some, this was at the Front, for others in the factory or field. Yet they all did their bit. And today we all enjoy, sometimes take for granted, the freedom their contribution guaranteed.

"Business leaders, locally and nationally, helped to marshal people, ideas and resources to innovate in many different ways, in many different sectors. And this provided a vital support to our troops, and to our citizens at home, by being the stable, dependable entity that people needed. Their legacy is an inspiration to us all." ■

The Post Office: standing firm and carrying on

The Post Office played a major role in preserving the normal functioning of the home front, in promoting the domestic war effort and in military operations.

At the outbreak of war, the Post Office was the largest employer in the country. Yet by 1942 it had lost one-third of its work force to active service. Females replaced male workers in very large numbers.

The organisation played a crucial role in preserving national and international communications in wartime, yet had to do so despite not only the need to recruit and train new staff, but also the destruction by bombing of postal and sorting offices and their staff, and of telephone cables.

The task of maintaining communications was all the more difficult due to the movement of population through mobilisation, evacuation and the effects of bombing. In fact, in July 1941 staff were issued with the following instructions regarding what to do in the event of an invasion: "All members of the staff must know that it is their duty to STAND FIRM and to CARRY ON with their normal vocations along with the rest of the civilian population, unless they are definitely instructed to the contrary."

From August 1940, Dover was in range of the German army's long-range guns in France. Yet, in an account of the time written by the head postmaster there: "Many of the homes of members of staff have been badly damaged... yet in no case has Hitler been cited as an excuse for failure to report for duty."

The Post Office soon acquired new, war-related tasks, including the distribution of ration books and public information leaflets, and the organisation of war savings. As a consequence of the war, many more people qualified for pensions and allowances payable through the Post Office.

The Post Office also had to ensure that mail reached service personnel overseas, another essential contribution to wartime morale. Even more crucially to the outcome of the war, Post Office engineers made an indispensable contribution to breaking the German Enigma Code.

In addition, their work in increasing the size of the telegraph network three-fold made possible the military communications that were vital to the success of the D-Day landings. The invasion force relied totally on communications laid by engineers, as was reported by the Director General: "The telegraph network... was three times as extensive as the whole pre-war civil telegraph network. The mileage of trunk telephone lines made available to them was greater than that of the whole trunk network available for public use at the outbreak of war."

The resourcefulness and determined resistance to the war by workers in the postal service helped to exemplify the popular image of the 'plucky British'.

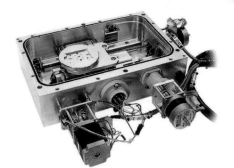

The power of invention

Paul Beaver takes a look at the technological innovations that enabled Britain to win the war

Technology has been a war-winner since before history was recorded: bronze weapons won over those made of wood or iron; English longbows defeated the armoured knights of medieval France; cannon against cavalry or machine guns against ranks of attacking infantry. But in World War II (WWII), it was not just weapons of war that made victory possible against the Nazi tyranny.

Fighting the submarine war, the British naval escorts were equipped first with underwater sensors, mounted on warship hulls, to detect German and Italian submarines with a sound-locating device, then with a sound-ranging device, sonar. Meanwhile, above water, the boffins developed a system of radio-ranging and detection, a British invention that helped save the country in the Battle of Britain (July-October 1940) and now known as radar.

In 1940, the home chain of radar stations along the east and south coasts of England detected enemy bomber raids building up over France and the Low Countries, enabling the meagre resources of Fighter Command to be positioned to meet the incoming raids.

Even as the Luftwaffe bombers were attacking southern England on an almost hourly basis, the boffins were hard at work creating smaller and smaller radar sets to be carried on warships and aircraft.

The first warship equipped was the new aircraft carrier HMS *Illustrious*, later joined by a host of warships, including battleships (for ranging the guns) and cruisers (for detecting the enemy). As the technology was improved, radar was developed for anti-submarine warfare, allowing the escorts to use the system to spot submarine periscopes breaking the surface.

By late 1944, maritime reconnaissance aircraft of Royal Air Force (RAF) Coastal Command were equipped with anti-surface vessel radar (ASVR) that allowed even the small image of a periscope to be detected. Aircraft like the

POLES ON THE FRONTS

in World War II

Poland was the only country to fight in the European theatre of war from the first to the last day of the greatest armed conflict in the history of mankind. World War Two began with dual invasions of Poland, first by Nazi Germany on September 1st 1939 and, soon after, by the Soviet Union on September 17th 1939. Despite defeat in 1939, Poles went on formed five armies, including four in exile: in France in 1939, in the United Kingdom in 1940 and twice in the USSR: in 1941 (moved to the Middle East in 1942) and 1943. Thus, Poles fought on all fronts in the Second World War: in the West, in the East and at home.

Air Forces: Polish pilots played a most distinguished role in 1940 during the decisive Battle of Britain. The role of foreign airmen, of whom Poles formed the largest group with 145 pilots, cannot be overstated. They fought both in British and Polish squadrons and from 1940 to 1945 achieved 621 confirmed kills.

Navy: Just before the outbreak of war three Polish destroyers (Blyskawica, Burza and Grom) left for Great Britain. Later on they were joined by the submarines Orzel and Wilk which had managed to escape the Germans. From 1940 onwards the Polish Navy was expanded with ships leased from the Royal Navy and in 1945 it amounted to 4000 seamen on 15 ships. Polish vessels participated in many operations, culminating in the Normandy landings (Operation Overlord). In total, they participated in 665 battles and escorted 787 convoys, sunk 12 enemy ships (including 5 submarines) and 41 merchant vessels and damaged 24 more (including 8 submarines).

Army: Following the defeat of France in 1940, the Carpathian Riflemen Brigade left Syria and joined British forces in Egypt. About 20,000 men managed to withdraw from France to Great Britain. They formed the 1st Polish Corps to defend the eastern coast of Scotland, and the 1st Independent Parachute Brigade. Meanwhile, forces moving from the Soviet Union to the Middle East formed the 2nd Polish Corps under the command of General W. Anders. In December 1943 and January 1944 it was deployed in Italy and in May 1944 captured the hill and monastery of Monte Cassino.

In July 1944 the 1st Armoured Division (under the command of Gen. S. Maczek) was moved to France. It formed a part of the Canadian Corps and won fame in the battles of Falaise and Chambois (August 1944) where it closed the 'cauldron', helping cut off the retreating German divisions. When the war in Europe was coming to an end, Polish troops fighting at the side of the Western Allies numbered more than 210,000 soldiers.

Intelligence: It has a very special place in the Polish contribution to the Allies' war effort. On July 25, 1939, before the war began, the Poles provided Great Britain and France with one complete working copy each of the German coding machine 'Enigma', allowing the Allies to read secret German messages. The most spectacular achievement of the Polish Home Army intelligence during the war was a thorough study of the research centre and factory in Pennemuende, where V1 and V2 missiles were produced. The achievements of Polish military intelligence have been recounted in the report of the Anglo-Polish Historical Committee 'Intelligence Co-operation between Poland and Great Britain during World War II", published in May 2005.

The Polish resistance is widely known under the name Armia Krajowa (AK - Home Army). In the spring of 1944 it numbered more than 300,000 sworn soldiers. The Home Army to a large extent engaged the German forces through organised acts of sabotage and through open combat (in particular the Warsaw Uprising of 1944).

In the East: In 1943 Stalin decided to organise Polish armed forces to fight alongside the Red Army all the way to Berlin. At the end of the war they amounted to more than 330,000 soldiers formed in two armies.

In all, up to 2 millions Poles served between September 1st 1939 and May 8th 1945 in all the Polish military formations - regular forces, partisan troops and underground forces. In the final stage of war regular Polish troops on all the European fronts amounted to some 600,000 soldiers (army, air force and navy). Thus the Poles raised one of the largest armies of the victorious coalition.

WWW.WW2.PL

"It really was considered the life"

David Musther was a fighter pilot in North Africa and Italy in 1944-45.

As a Flight Lieutenant in 112 Squadron, his activities were to carry sizeable bombs to give the army support across the western desert and Italy. David explains: "Every day was different in a way. Most days it was to target tanks and troop concentrations that were holding up the army – mainly to order activity rather than big operations".

He does recall one operation – Operation Bowler. The plan was to bomb Venice Harbour because the Germans were bringing in fuel across the Adriatic at night and distributing it across Italy. David recalls: "It was a big operation, about 80 aircraft. It was called Bowler because the flight commander said, 'if it goes wrong I shall get my bowler hat and it will be the end of my career!'" The operation was, however, a success and no damage was done to the city.

"There was a fairly heavy cost to that type of work because we flew low and we flew into targets and every target was well defended so we lost a lot of guys – it was the nature of the job," he explains.

"My memories are in some ways sad, but in many ways joyful in terms of the people I met and the work we did. For young men it really was considered the life!"

Sonar and radar turned the tide of the Battle of the Atlantic

Shorts Sunderland Flying Boat – known to U-Boats as the 'flying porcupine' because of its armaments – became the scourge of the Bay of Biscay, as they were able to detect and engage submarines on the surface or just below. Sonar and radar also turned the tide of the Battle of the Atlantic (1939-1943).

On another front, the strategic bombing of Germany called for advanced technology in navigation and marking targets. The Air Ministry in London, together with the research establishments at Boscombe Down (Wiltshire), Farnborough (Hampshire) and Martlesham Heath (East Anglia), worked on perfecting new technology for taking bombers to their targets, even in the worst northwest European weather.

Bomber Command's first navigation device was called Gee and it relied on radio signals that were transmitted to send a network of Morse code across enemy-occupied Europe. The bomber-stream leader would follow the transmissions until the signals created a continuous pitch – that was overhead the target.

Marking the targets on the ground was the job of the Pathfinder Force, usually equipped with unarmed Mosquito high-speed bombers that carried target indicators that burned red or green. These markers were used as visual guides by the bomb-aimers of Lancaster, Halifax and Stirling bombers, known as the 'main force'. But these bombers were vulnerable. Again technology would come to their aid.

In 1943, RAF bombers en route to Hamburg were protected not by fighters or guns, but by thousands of pieces of tinfoil strips that fluttered to the ground. This radar-jamming system was cheap and easy to manufacture, but nevertheless high technology in its own right. Dropped in bundles by bombers intent on creating a diversion, the tinfoil strips slowly floated to earth creating the impression on German radar screens that hundreds of bombers were in the area. German night-fighters would

Not only did equipment improve, medical advances were made that saved countless lives

The Guinea Pig Club

The Guinea Pig Club is a group consisting mainly of fighter pilots burned in their aeroplanes during the Battle of Britain, who were treated by Sir Archibald McIndoe at the Queen Victoria Hospital in East Grinstead, West Sussex and later at Rooksdown, Basingstoke in Hampshire.

The Guinea Pigs were given this name simply because Sir Archibald had no choice but to try out his treatments on the men, as there was no medical reference book to guide him.

Recovering pilots set up the Club themselves in July 1941. Their sense of humour can be seen in the name of the club and in the first appointments: the first secretary had had his fingers seriously burned so any notes of club meetings had to be short, while the first treasurer was a pilot with very badly burned legs – so he could not run away with the club's funds!

Sir Archibald (also known by colleagues as 'The Boss' or 'The Maestro') did not limit his work to a medical/physical level. He realised that the injured pilots needed some form of psychological rehabilitation and he did his best to facilitate this. After the war, he received many awards for his work. During the war he was awarded a CBE, and he was knighted in 1947.

By the end of the war, the total number of Guinea Pigs stood at 649; 57 per cent were British and the rest from the Commonwealth. Surviving members of the Club endeavour to meet each year and, since the death of Sir Archibald McIndoe in 1960, the Duke of Edinburgh has been the Club's president.

be directed to the area to find nothing, as complete chaos ensued among the ground defences while the night-fighters' airborne-radar also went 'on the blink'.

RAF night-fighters were also equipped with airborne radar. Based initially at RAF Middle Wallop in Hampshire, the first radar-equipped Bristol Beaufighter aircraft defended the industrial Midlands. To protect the technology in the Beaufighter's 'thimble' nose, the early successes were put down to the pilots eating carrots. The squadron commander was nicknamed 'Cat's Eyes' by the Ministry of Information, a nickname, incidentally, that the late Group Captain John Cunningham heartily disliked for the next 50 years.

Technology, driven by the needs of national survival, abounded on the land fronts as well. Not only did personal equipment improve, medical advances were made that saved countless lives and, of course, weapons of war.

Landing on the beaches of Normandy in June 1944, British and Canadian troops were supported by the 'Hobart Funnies'. These were a series of specially-converted Sherman tanks that included mine-destroying flails, flame-throwers and engineer vehicles – the forerunners of today's armoured fighting vehicles. Meanwhile, artillery increased its firepower, rifles became more accurate and vehicles were more reliable and better protected.

Then there was the 'greatest' technology of all: the atomic bomb. History records that American and British scientists worked for three years to create 'instant sunshine' in the form of a weapon of mass destruction. It was used just twice, against cities in Japan that have become infamous: Hiroshima and Nagasaki. Whatever the rights and wrongs of such destructive power, the weapon is credited with ending WWII. ■

Staying on track

The UK's railway network was an essential form of transport during the conflict. **Christian Wolmar** discovers how it fared under the constant barrage of enemy bombs

Transport and communications are vital in a war and, therefore, railways are extremely vulnerable to enemy bombing. At the time of World War II (WWII), the railways, rather than the roads, were still the principal form of transport for both goods and people. Hence, Britain's rail network was a natural target for attack by German aircraft.

However, thanks to the efforts of the railway workers and the co-operation of the public, the railways proved resilient and largely remained functioning throughout WWII, apart from some localised damage.

This resilience also reflected the lack of a consciously planned national rail network. A cluster of private companies, thinking more inter-regionally than nationally, laid the foundations of a system in the 19th century, which decades later provided significant opportunities for re-routing trains around bomb-damaged track.

As in World War I, the government quickly commandeered the railways, which were still owned privately, soon after war was declared. This time, unlike previously, there was a bar on railway workers being called up for military service, because the government realised that they were of more use running the railways than serving in the forces, which showed how important the network was to the war effort.

Immediately on the declaration of war in the summer of 1939, the railways were put to intensive use for the evacuation of children into the countryside. This was a very successful long-planned operation with hundreds of thousands of children being quickly transferred away from London and other big cities. Hospital patients were also sent out of cities in ambulance trains, which had been specially prepared for the purpose.

The railways were also quickly called into action to aid troop movements. The soldiers of the expeditionary force that crossed the Channel in 1940, and soon returned defeated from Dunkirk, were transported to and from the ports by rail. Again, the railways coped with the enormous increase in traffic with little problem.

Under fire

Heavy bombing started later that year, which, at times, was aimed specifically at railway stations and depots. Lines were disrupted, often for days at a time, and London's Waterloo station suffered particularly badly: on one occasion all of its signalling was put out of action. Yet, in true fighting spirit, railwaymen helped by volunteers used flags to shepherd the trains in and out of the huge station.

On one terrible night in May 1941, seven London stations were put out of action by bombing and it took a month to restore a full service at Waterloo, which was the most badly damaged. While the attacks died down towards the end of that year, the railways faced a new danger in 1944: the flying-bomb attacks.

Despite all the attacks and damage, the railways kept functioning, to such an extent that more people were being carried during WWII than in peacetime. Indeed, such was the demand that by 1944 there were two-thirds more passengers than in 1938.

The railways were asked to provide dozens of special troop trains every day, a number that increased as preparations for the invasion of France (D-Day, June 1944) were being made. However, amazingly, the railways also continued to run nearly all of the regular passenger services.

Travelling by train could be a slightly perilous business, especially at night. Trains were blacked-out at night and light bulbs were painted dark blue, giving out just enough of a glow to enable passengers to avoid sitting on already-occupied seats. Station lights, of course, were all turned off and a white line was

Working the trams

David Prince, now 94, worked on the trams and buses in Liverpool during the war. He remembers an occasion when he was about to take the tram down James Street. "A chap came up to me and said 'you don't want to go down there – there's a big hole in the middle of the road!'"

Often the tram was made to go on huge detours or completely stopped because the overhead wires were down, or because an air raid was taking place. David recalls: "During the bombings I had to stop and find shelter in the nearest pub. I went to more strange pubs at that time than I've ever known!"

Louise Drew

UNDERGROUND

If attacked, drivers would try to get to a tunnel to hide, or speed up to try to outpace attacking planes

painted to show passengers where to disembark. However, that did not stop one poor man trying to alight at Bath, from a coach that had stopped before the platform, only to find himself plunging off the viaduct into the River Avon. Amazingly, he lived to tell the tale.

Trains travelling through the countryside were, at times, a specific target for German bombers and fighter planes. Although some locomotives were armour plated, most were completely defenceless and vulnerable to such attacks. If attacked, drivers would try to get to a tunnel to hide, or speed up to try to outpace attacking planes.

Locomotives were the key targets, but one German plane made the mistake of being too near its quarry after a successful attack and was downed when the engine's boiler blew up. On several occasions trains plunged into recently created bomb craters, but mostly this was at slow speed and, surprisingly, there were few deaths from such incidents.

Probably the most famous image of the railways during WWII is the sight of thousands of people sheltering from the Blitz in the London Underground. It is important to emphasise that the Underground kept running throughout. At first, the authorities were reluctant to let people stay overnight, but eventually people-power won and Herbert Morrison, when he became Home Secretary, ensured that the tunnels and stations were opened up to all comers.

Remarkably, the Underground only suffered three direct hits during the Blitz, and while 152 were killed, there is no doubt that thousands of lives were saved. It was precisely because of their good record

Strict blackout conditions meant that cars drove with tiny side-lights

that the Tube tunnels became known as 'the best shelters of all'.

Ironically, the worst Underground incident was not caused by enemy action but by a stampede, caused by a false alarm, at Bethnal Green in March 1943. Tragically, 173 people, mainly women and children, suffocated in the single entrance to the station.

At times, up to 175,000 people sheltered in the Underground system, with the authorities providing special food trains selling tea, buns and sandwiches. They also ensured there was adequate sanitation, which proved to be a major problem during the first few weeks, and even laid on entertainment with singers and variety acts at some of the stations.

Given the intensity and length of attacks, and how exposed the railways were, it is remarkable that only 400 railway workers and 180 London Transport staff were killed by enemy action, along with an estimated 600 passengers.

Nevertheless, the war left the railways in a miserable state because investment plans had been shelved to concentrate on the war effort. Much equipment, including 14,000 passenger carriages, a third of the stock, had been damaged or destroyed. This led the government to decide that there was no alternative other than nationalisation – the creation of British Railways in 1948 can be said to be a direct consequence of WWII.

The roads were obviously also a vital form of transport, but with petrol rationing and a shortage of vehicles – many were commandeered by the army – few ordinary people could use them. Given the shortage of petrol, wherever possible even the army ensured that material and men were transported by trains, which were fuelled by coal, which, unlike oil, was available in abundant supply in the UK.

Despite the relatively light traffic, road deaths reached an all time high of 9,000 a year – compared to 3,500 today – because of the strictly enforced blackout conditions, which meant that cars drove with just tiny side-lights or no lighting at all. White strips were painted on the streetlights, which were turned off, to help drivers see them.

Roads were not often a target for enemy action, though many did suffer bomb damage and vehicles occasionally plunged into huge craters caused by air raid attacks. ■

Singapore Remembers

We are privileged to contribute to this commemorative publication as a tribute to the courage, resilience and dedication of all those who struggled to preserve the cause of freedom during the Second World War.

We in Singapore have particular reason to be thankful. Thousands of British and Allied military and civilian personnel died during the defence of Singapore. Nearly 150,000 people were incarcerated between 1942-1945, including over 100,000 troops and the entire European civilian population of Singapore. The local population including Chinese, Malays, Indians and Eurasians also suffered horrendous depredations.

When Lord Mountbatten accepted the surrender of 680,000 Japanese forces in South East Asia on 12th September 1945, it marked the end of the war in the Asia Pacific. The joy and relief of those who survived was suffused with sorrow for those who had lost their lives.

Singaporeans have never forgotten those dark times. As every year passes so the need grows to remember those who fought alongside our own people so that we could live in peace. This year, the sixtieth anniversary of the end of World War II, is no exception.

Kranji War Memorial

On 15th February we remembered the day in 1942 that Singapore fell, with a service in the War Memorial Park. In September we will honour those who fought the final battle at Pasir Panjang and the last stand of the Malay regiment at Bukit Chandu by inviting members of the public to follow the trail of these events of 14th and 15th February 1942.

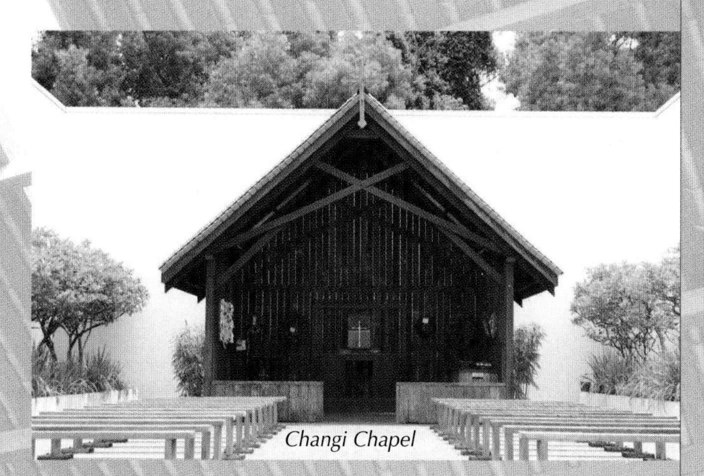

Changi Chapel

On 8th September we will lay a commemorative plaque at Fort Siloso accompanied by a gun salute to those responsible for Singapore's defences. On 10th September we remember those who were incarcerated, with a memorial service at Changi Chapel followed by the opening of a new exhibition of works by wartime artists and original artefacts from prison life. Special access to the Changi Murals, evocative wall paintings by the British POW Stanley Warren, will also be available to those on guided tours during this period.

On 11th September, a new memorial will be dedicated at Sembawang, site of the former naval base, to the memory of the crews of Force "Z" of the Royal Navy who sailed to confront the Japanese invasion fleet off Kota Bahru. The sinking of the two capital ships, HMS Prince of Wales and HMS Repulse, with the loss of many lives was a turning point in the battle to defend Singapore.

Our commemorations end fittingly at dawn on 12th September, 60 years to the day when the war ended in the Asia Pacific, with our annual Dedication Service at Kranji War Memorial where most of the fallen are buried. On the memorial are the words; 'They died for all free men'.

As, in our respective countries, we give thanks for our future by commemorating the past, let us re-dedicate ourselves to the cause of peace and liberty, for which so many gave their lives.

WWW.VISITSINGAPORE.COM/WWII

There can be little doubt of the immense contribution that civil defence made to the British war effort

In defence of the realm

Defending our people

Unlike all previous wars, civilians were in the front line in WWII. Roger J.C. Thomas explores the vital role that civil defence played in the war effort

Most of us have enjoyed watching *Dad's Army* on television; famed for taking a gentle dig at the Home Guard, it is also memorable for Bill Pertwee's depiction of the sour-faced, white-helmeted and very belligerent Chief Warden Hodges.

Like all of the characters of *Dad's Army*, Hodges was a caricature – a synthesis of numerous wardens who rigorously enforced the wartime blackout, bellowing the time-honoured phrase: "Put that light out!" As with any caricature, this was an over simplification of reality, but it has kept civil defence alive in our country's consciousness.

The civil defence organisation was born out of the painful experiences of the bombing of London during World War I (WWI). It was realised that by taking the simple precaution of establishing a blackout, providing air-raid shelters and adequate warning of an attack, the number of casualties incurred in a raid could be substantially reduced.

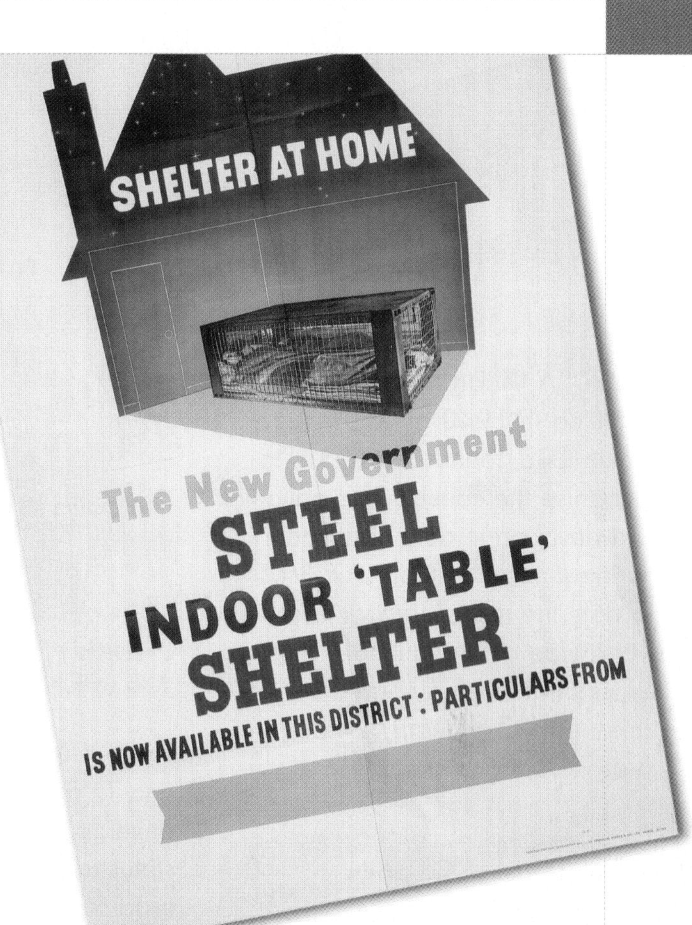

SHELTER AT HOME
The New Government
STEEL
INDOOR 'TABLE'
SHELTER
IS NOW AVAILABLE IN THIS DISTRICT: PARTICULARS FROM

Necessary precautions

In 1929, the Committee of Imperial Defence was established to examine a variety of issues, including passive or civil defence, but it took the growth of militarism in Nazi Germany to persuade the Home Office to establish Air Raid Precautions (ARP) in 1935, directed by Wing Commander Hodsell.

Hodsell quickly set about organising a national system of civil defence: an anti-gas school was opened at Falfield in Gloucestershire; a gas-mask factory was started in a converted cotton mill near Blackburn; and a school of civil defence was opened at Easingwold, Yorkshire.

The ARP Act was passed by Parliament in 1937, making it a statutory requirement for councils to make provisions for civil defence in their communities. If anyone had doubts about this policy, the Munich Crisis of 1938 dispelled them and gave added impetus to the supply of gas masks and domestic air-raid shelters. The provision of air-raid shelters was means-tested and families with an annual income of

"Golly, I got two already"

In 1940, when Britain stood alone, Kitty Burr and her friend Sylv prepared to do their bit. They were single girls in the 'luxury trade' of hairdressing and were sent away to work at an Elstree factory, making bomb doors for the Halifax four-engined bomber.

It was a labour of love for Kitty, as her brother had been called up to the Royal Air Force; as it happens, he survived the war as a Halifax rear gunner.

"When we arrived at the billet the landlady opened the door with iron rollers in her hair and her hands crossed across her stomach and said: 'Golly, I got two already.' The only thing she could give us was a double-bed in a tiny room, which we had to shuffle round to get in."

And the four girls had less than a pint-and-a-half of hot water to share between them in the morning. But life also had its ups: as a member of the most productive manufacturing team, Kitty won an unforgettable flight in the bomber she was helping to build.

Paul Beaver

Acknowledging the role of animals

PDSA, the UK's leading veterinary charity

The PDSA Dickin Medal was instituted in 1943 by Maria Dickin CBE, founder of PDSA, to recognise the conspicuous gallantry and devotion to duty of animals during times of military conflict. To date the medal, recognised worldwide as 'the animals' Victoria Cross', has been awarded sixty times – to 32 pigeons, 24 dogs, three horses and a cat.

Winkie receiving the PDSA Dickin Medal from Maria Dickin CBE

The first recipient was a homing pigeon, Winkie, whose escape from a ditched aircraft led to the crew being rescued. Canine heroes included Rob the para dog, who completed more than 20 parachute descents with the SAS, and Jet, who served with London's Civil Defence Services to rescue people trapped under blitzed buildings.

Rob with his regiment

The PDSA Dickin Medal serves not only to acknowledge the role of animals but also to raise their status in society. This and the eradication of animal suffering were Maria Dickin's aims from the time she founded PDSA in 1917 and they remain the core of PDSA philosophy today.

With 42 PDSA PetAid hospitals, 4 PDSA PetAid branches and more than 300 PDSA PetAid practices providing free treatment to the sick and injured pets of people in need, PDSA continues to fulfil a vital role in ensuring the health and wellbeing of the nation's companion animals.

> *"To date the PDSA Dickin Medal, widely recognised as 'the animals' Victoria Cross', has been awarded sixty times."*

To find out if you qualify for free PDSA veterinary care, **freephone 0800 731 2502**.

For ways you can help PDSA **freephone 0800 917 2509**.

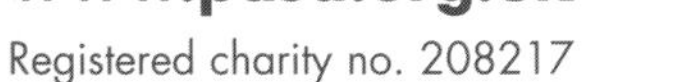

www.pdsa.org.uk

Registered charity no. 208217

"We could have both of us been killed"

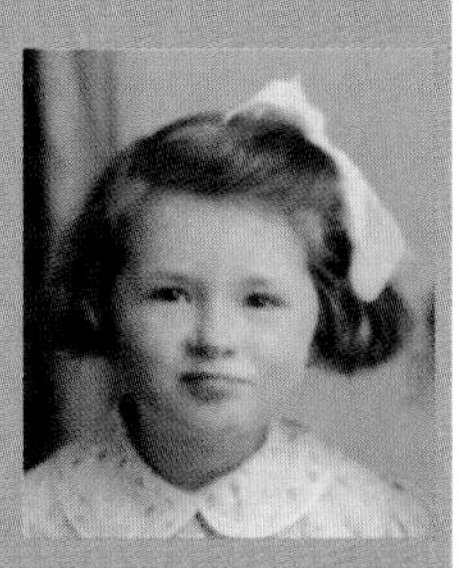

Simone Lightfoot was three years old when the war started. She grew up in Brentford, West London, with her mother and younger sister. She has vivid memories of several terrifying air raids throughout 1943-45, and of nights spent huddled with her family in the Anderson shelter at the bottom of the garden.

"A bomb fell on the pavement while I was going to the newsagents with my aunt. It actually fell as we were walking along – there was no warning at all. This was in the middle of the day. It left a massive crater in the road – we could have both of us been killed.

"We always had to carry a gas mask with us. Everybody wore them, so you just accepted it. They had a horrible smell – I can still smell it today.

"One night, they started dropping incendiary bombs. This time we were in the house and we didn't have time to get down to the shelter. Once the bombs started falling, that was it, we just had to wait in the house. I was so nervous, I started screaming, I just couldn't stop, I was so petrified."

Howard Gossington

less than £250 could receive either an Anderson or a Morrison Shelter, free.

The people's army

On the outbreak of war in 1939, civil defence was manned predominantly by civilian volunteers. Great Britain was divided into 12 civil defence regions, each supervised by a Regional Commissioner. Thankfully, during the so-called 'phoney war', the civil defence teams were only occasionally called upon. However, the relative calm was shattered in 1940, when they found themselves thrust into the maelstrom of the German bombing campaign, facing the dangers of unexploded bombs (UXBs), incendiaries, un-safe buildings, burst gas mains and live electrical cables.

Towns and villages were divided into ARP sectors, monitored by ARP wardens' posts. The posts were usually sited within strengthened basements or in purpose-built blast-proof shelters that were connected by telephone to a control centre and were equipped with stirrup pumps, fire buckets, rescue equipment and first aid boxes.

The wardens at each post were responsible for a number of streets, usually with a population of about 500. In addition to the wardens, each post had a number of volunteer 'runners', usually young boys, who would deliver messages by hand if the telephones were down.

The post acted as a point of contact for the public where they could receive advice on blackout regulations, gas

There is little doubt of the contribution that civil defence made to the war

masks, shelter, food and water, re-housing and tracing missing persons.

A warden was usually the first official to arrive at an incident, he had to assess the harrowing scenes of shattered homes among the clouds of dust, smoke and the smell of destruction; all the time at risk of death or injury to himself.

His report would contain information on the location of an incident, the number of people trapped or injured, damage to roads, gas or water mains, and if possible, the type of bomb involved, or whether there were any UXBs nearby.

Although the wardens were the front line, their role was just a small part of the organisation. Once the control centre had a clear idea of an incident, they would send specialist civil defence workers, these could include rescue parties, sniffer dogs, heavy lift crews, mobile first aid parties, stretcher parties, the Auxiliary Ambulance Service, the National Fire Service (NFS), repair and demolition crews, and even the Women's Voluntary Service (WVS) to provide succour both to the residents and to the civil defence teams themselves.

On one particular occasion, in September 1940, the WVS even mounted a major evacuation of thousands of people trapped by a massive fire in the Surrey Docks.

Civil defence also managed a range of rather mundane roles that rarely gained recognition. For example, most bomb-damaged homes were quickly made wind- and weather-proof. Admittedly these were temporary repairs, using heavy-gauge waxed brown paper instead of glass and corrugated sheeting on roofs, but it did enable people to stay in their own homes.

Where people were temporarily homeless, the WVS, the Salvation Army, and other similar organisations ran more than 10,000 rest centres to provide a refuge. When large numbers of people were affected by loss of power or water supplies, the local civil defence committees could call upon all manner of mobile services, including canteens, tea cars, food convoys, mobile laundries and shower-bath units. Remarkably, even animal welfare was considered, tended by the National ARP Animals' Committee (NARPAC).

There can be little doubt of the immense contribution that civil defence made to the British war effort throughout the Blitz, and later during the German V-bomb offensive. The presence of an efficient rescue service helped to maintain morale during the darkest times and thousands of lives were saved that otherwise would have been lost. Recognition of the role played by the men and women of the ARP was given in 1941, in a book titled *Civil Defence in War*:

"The People's Army is an army of equality, in which men and women, rich and poor, young and old, are working side by side." ■

Hitler's terror weapons

"The noise was incredible, unbearable and I was so scared." The memories of the wartime bombing raids are the same for many thousands of people across the United Kingdom's home front. From Exeter to Aberdeen, Belfast to Dover, the Luftwaffe aerial bombardment raged from 1940 until it petered out in 1944.

Then, rather than respite, Hitler unleashed the secret aerial weapons, the so-called 'terror weapons' of the V1 Doodle Bug and the V2 Rocket. "We somehow felt safer with the Doodle Bug," remembers Norman Beaver, a Home Guard by night and munitions worker by day.

"As long as you could hear the motor, you were safe. But when it cut out, the bomb came crashing down and exploded with a huge crash." For those who were under the flight path of the V2 rocket, there was no comfort of the droning motor, just the blinding flash of the warhead.

Paul Beaver

Defending our shores

During the war, Britain's land and coastline was a brutal patchwork of barbed wire, tank traps, anti-invasion blocks and pillboxes. **William Foot** looks at the steps Britain took to secure its freedom

After the defeat of the British Expeditionary Force (BEF) in France, in June 1940, and the miraculous return of some 200,000 of our troops from Dunkirk (plus 100,000 French), for the first time in nearly 150 years Britain had to face up to the imminent threat of invasion. Such an invasion would have resulted in a ground war to decide not only the fate of the nation, but the British Empire and, very likely, the entire free world.

Britain's defence had for centuries lain with the Royal Navy, but from the 1930s it had increasingly been the Royal Air Force and the developing technology of air warfare in which we entrusted our security. Our ground defences were limited principally to coastal batteries to protect ports and dockyards. As the 'phoney war' ended with the German's Blitzkrieg (Lightning War) invasion of France, a programme of Emergency Coast Defence Batteries was rushed into effect with some 50 batteries, equipped mainly with 6in guns stripped from World War I battleships, set up on vulnerable stretches of Britain's east and south coasts. Over the next year, the number of these batteries doubled.

Ground defences

The threat to Britain was intensified after the defeat of France and the occupation of the Channel coast. Earlier, the main threat had been considered to be from an attack across the North Sea. Now Hitler's forces lay only 20 miles away across a narrow strip of water. Under Germany's Operation Sea Lion plans, an invading armada would have attacked the English coast from Thanet to the Isle of Wight.

While the BEF was returning from Dunkirk, General Sir Edmund Ironside was appointed Commander-in-Chief Home Forces. He had the enormous job of organising Britain for the ground defence of her own homeland, with severely depleted resources: most of the army's guns, tanks, and vehicles had been left at Dunkirk and the returning troops had to be rested, reorganised and retrained.

In June 1940, for the defence of some 400 miles of coastline, the British Army had only 15 undermanned infantry divisions, plus one incomplete armoured division. These troops had a fraction of the weapons they should have possessed. For instance, only 100 2lb anti-tank guns, which had in any case proved ineffective against the German tanks in France, and 2,500 Bren guns (the Army's principal light-machine-gun). Nevertheless, against this background, the construction of the greatest system of ground defences this country has ever seen was about to begin.

General Ironside's priority was the defence of the coastline. The Germans were to be denied the level beaches they needed on which to land and the ports through which they could bring their supplies. The shoreline was defended by 'obstacles': fire trenches and other earthworks, barbed wire, minefields, concrete blocks, machine gun posts and concrete pillboxes, with artillery to the rear. From 1941, hundreds of miles of tubular-beachwood scaffolding were added to the coastal defences.

Natural protection

Inland, the countryside, in particular that of the south east of England, was divided up by a network of stop lines and other defence lines, the aim of which was to

"The king demanded to be allowed on board"

Welshman John Brooks was an air mechanic with the Royal Navy for the duration of the war, based on aircraft carriers HMS *Perseus* and later HMS *Implacable*.

John recalls an occasion that stands out as somewhat bizarre, but was in many ways reassuring to both himself and the rest of his crew that some things did not change in times of war.

"At about 10.00am, one day during November 1944, my ship, aircraft carrier HMS *Perseus*, was on route from Singapore to Sydney and fast approaching the equator. Suddenly the ship was stopped after being hailed by a small boat, in which there were five men. One was a large, stout person dressed in odd-looking robes and wearing a crown, who was accompanied by an equally odd-looking mate as 'queen' and three burly looking individuals known as 'bears'.

The king (Neptune) demanded to be allowed on board to meet the captain and service officers – this was agreed to and Neptune asked for all the ship's company to be assembled on deck. Neptune seated himself on a chair alongside a freshly erected swimming pool.

"He then read out a list of misdemeanours of the ship's company and pronounced the punishment – invariably to be shoved in the swimming pool. The first person to be chosen by the king was placed in a collapsible chair over the pool and lathered with a large paintbrush and noxious soap, then tipped backwards into the pool where the three bears ducked him 10 times, in-between tossing him in the air.

"This went on until all members of the crew, officers and mates alike, who had never crossed the equator before, were similarly treated. All would be excused further treatment by King Neptune forever." Although it was a strange experience, John says it was "a pleasant reminder that the Royal Navy could still carry out ancient traditions, even though we were still at war".

Louise Drew

prevent the German armoured forces breaking out into the heart of the country, as they had done in France.

Many of the stop lines followed rivers that provided an anti-tank obstacle. However, where such a natural obstacle was unavailable, artificial anti-tank ditches – 10ft-deep and 15ft-wide – were dug, or lines of 6ft-high concrete blocks erected.

Natural crossing-points, such as roads and railways, were protected by pillboxes and anti-tank gun emplacements – the latter were sometimes armed with a 6lb gun, last used in WWI. Meanwhile, hundreds of bridges were rigged with explosives.

Bolstering the defence of these linear anti-tank barriers was a system of fortifications known as 'nodal points'. These had all-round defences that protected road junctions and railways, and were usually manned by the Home Guard (formed in mid-May 1940 and originally named the Local Defence Volunteers). Some nodal points had defences to withstand attack by armoured vehicles and were known as anti-tank islands. Characteristic of the defences was a roadblock with barriers formed by concrete obstacles and steel rails, set vertically or horizontally, across the carriageway.

The countryside was divided up by a network of stop lines

The roadblocks were generally overlooked by a pillbox, a concrete structure that became iconic of 1940s defence. They were often hexagonal in shape, but could also be square or rectangular, and sometimes had an open-roof-area designed for anti-aircraft fire. Another weapon employed by the Home Guard was the flame fougasse, which was normally set in roadside banks where a mixture of petrol and tar would be detonated to create a wall of flame.

"I was only 14 and I knew I was going to die"

Charles Evans was a dockworker in Merseyside, Liverpool during the war.

He recalls an experience that could very nearly have been his last:

"At the beginning of the war I worked on the LMS Railway and on many nights an air raid would start as I walked home. I was on the way home one night, from the city centre to the suburbs, when an air raid started. ! ran to the air raid shelter but the entrance was blocked with people and I couldn't get in. I heard a terrible tearing noise and I knew it was going to drop just there. I put my hands up to my eyes – I was only 14 and I knew I was going to die. The bomb fell and struck the cornice of a building just 20ft away... how about that? It didn't explode!"

Charles also recalls a similar situation that happened to a ship – *West Kedron* – that called in at the docks: "Halfway across the Atlantic they had been attacked by aircraft who opened fire with half-inch cannon shells. They then dropped a bomb, which struck the flying bridge, rolled beneath and skittered along the deck and then hit a cast iron bollard – yet still did not explode! The crew picked it up and threw it overboard."

Louise Drew

Blitzkrieg had taught Britain the danger of attack by airborne troops. Consequently, all open areas (that could provide a suitable landing-strip for enemy troop-carrying aircraft and gliders) within five miles of the coast or an airfield were rendered impassable. This was achieved by digging trenches across fields, parkland, and playing fields, or by positioning obstacles such as old motorcars across them. Even straight lengths of arterial roads were blocked.

The system of defence was organised by the Royal Engineers, much of the construction work of pillboxes and other gun emplacements being given to private contractors. As the weeks went by and the Germans did not come, so the defences became stronger, and the vital weapons and trained troops to man them began to build up.

General Ironside was replaced by General Alan Brooke, who further strengthened the coastal defence and built up powerful mobile forces. If the outcome of the Battle of Britain (the air-battle between the RAF and the Luftwaffe, July-October 1940) had been different, it would have been Brooke who commanded the land battles fought across the south of England.

The invasion threat continued into 1941, but by the spring of that year Britain was infinitely more capable of defending herself than she had been nine months earlier. Germany's invasion of Russia in June 1941 meant the effective end of Operation Sea Lion, in turn, Britain had secured its freedom and was now fully able to take the war to the enemy.

Although no ground fighting in Britain actually took place, the lines of pillboxes and 'dragon's teeth' that can still be seen across the countryside mark the high-water mark of Nazi expansion and provide a memorial to our nation's courage at this time of terrible danger. ■

The fierce air battles that took place overhead are keenly remembered as the key to preserving Britain's freedom. Yet, at the same time on the ground, plenty was being done to cause as much interference as possible to the incoming waves of German bombers, explains **Richard Morris**

Defending our skies

In 1939 there were about 176,000 people in the Royal Air Force (RAF). By war's end there were more than a million. With Anti-Aircraft (AA) Command and the Royal Observer Corps, defending the skies was a mass enterprise.

Despite that, we remember it selectively. This might be because quite a lot of what was specifically involved in this type of defence was secret at the time. Maybe, too, it reflects the extent to which film and literature influence what we recall.

In wartime and early post-war cinema, fighter-piloting tended to go with charisma, rather than oily maintenance. Most accounts of the aerial battles of 1940, and the night-time struggle that followed, were written by pilots.

Paul Richey's *Fighter Pilot* appeared in 1941. Richard Hillary's *The Last Enemy* was a bestseller from the day it was published in 1942. John Magee, who wrote *High Flight*, the sonnet that has since become a flyers' anthem, flew Spitfires. After the war came more books by or about pilots – figures such as Townsend, Cunningham and, most recently, Geoffrey Wellum.

Yet as John Terraine reflected at the end of his history of the Air Force in WWII, most of the RAF's million were ground crew. And without them, no aircraft would have flown.

Air Marshal Sir James Robb was appointed Commander-in-Chief Fighter Command a week after VE Day (May 8 1945). Without radar, he reflected, "The Battle of Britain, even the war itself, could not have been won." Yet, radar's existence had only just been publicly revealed.

Radar was the business of RAF 60 Group. When the Group's commander wrote to thank all ranks for what they had done, he told them: "Secrecy has meant that you could not talk to your friends about your work, that the press could not write about it as they did about many other Service activities of less importance, and that Commanders in Chief could not openly congratulate you on your work."

Radar was a result of one of several influential decisions that had been taken back in the 1930s. Another was to equip Fighter Command with swift, eight-gun monoplane fighters (the Spitfire and Hurricane, for example). A third was to reorganise the RAF into functional Commands. The three together gave a system of communication and control that enabled fighters to engage raiders, and alerted civil and anti-aircraft defences in endangered areas. The system was frugal – fighters did not roam at random, but were husbanded until needed, then directed to where needed most.

At first, however, there was little protection against attack by night. During the Night Blitz of 1940-41, bombers visited

"it was a tense experience"

Jack Millin flew with the South African Airforce as an air gunner and wireless operator.

Jack's job involved attacking selected targets in North Italy, such as troop concentrations, river and road bridges and railway junctions. He recalls: "It was a tense experience. I was only just 20 years old. But it was just part of the life of any air crew at the time."

He did, however, develop many unique friendships during his time serving in Italy, many of which still continue today. Jack is a member of the RAF South African Airforce, with 60 members from South Africa, UK, Australia, Botswana and Canada.

In fact, in September, thanks to money from the Big Lottery Fund, Jack will be re-visiting the three Italian bases he operated from during the war with other members from his order. He and 32 ex-servicemen, spouses and carers will be making the journey to Italy where there will be a service of remembrance held in Ancona.

Louise Drew

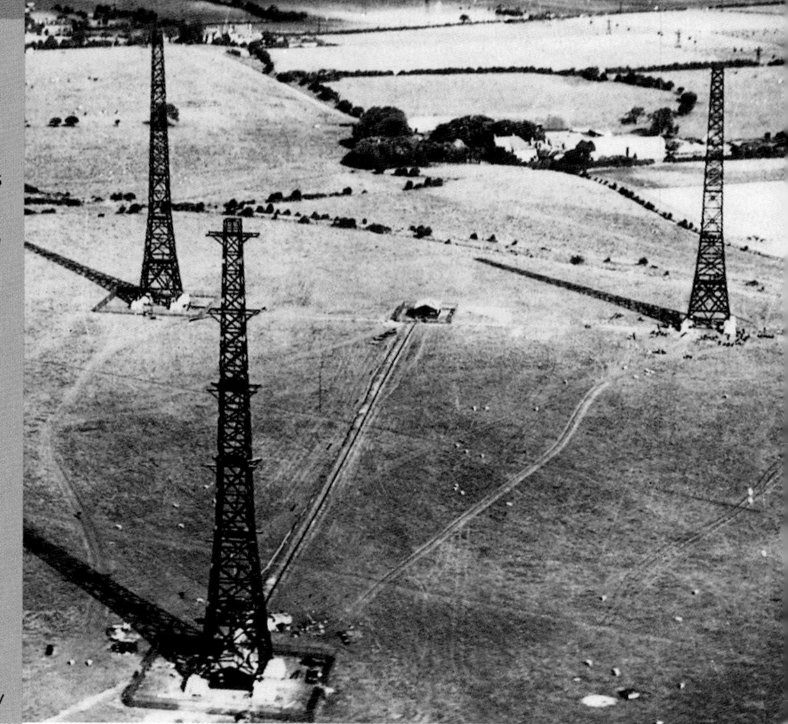

Balloon Command

Dame Laura Knight's painting *A Balloon Site*, Coventry, captures the physicality of handling a barrage balloon against the background of a Midlands landscape. The envelope was made of rubber-proofed cotton fabric. Filled with hydrogen, weighing about 250kg (550lbs) and flown on a steel cable, such balloons were used throughout the war to deter low-level attack on cities, ports and factories, and (latterly) as a form of static defence against flying bombs. Many were given nicknames by their crews.

By 1942 the British barrage had grown from hundreds to thousands and, as here, all-women crews carried out much of the work. The Ministry of Information, nonetheless, did its bit for male self-esteem by telling the public that this did not imply that men had previously been doing a "woman's job". On the contrary, "it is only the great progress in and simplification of balloon manipulation, for which the original officers and airmen of Balloon Command are responsible, that has made the substitution at all possible."

Richard Morris

cities more or less at will, while intruders stalked RAF aircraft around their home airfields. As months passed, however, tables were turned.

Tactics and trickery

Radar was again decisive. Gun-laying radar enabled AA fire to be aimed with increasing accuracy, while night-fighters equipped with airborne radar and guided by controllers on the ground became lethal hunters.

Others specialised in trickery. Among them were linguists of the Y-service, which eavesdropped on German radio traffic, and the RAF's 80 Wing, whose members worked to frustrate Knickebein – the Luftwaffe's radio-based system of direction for bombers – and to bewilder Luftwaffe aircrew by falsifying bearings from their navigational beacons.

Decoys of other kinds existed on the ground, where ingenious simulations were put in place to lure attackers away from their real targets. During the flying-bomb offensive in 1944, specious data about where some of the bombs fell were fed back to the Germans to upset their aim.

In much of this, women played a large part. By late-1944 there were nearly as many women in the Air Force as there had been men in 1939. Aside from occupations like radar where they were prominent all along, by 1942 over 1,000 barrage-balloon sites were staffed by Women's Auxiliary Air Force (WAAF) crews. In AA Command, a shortage of men prompted the formation of mixed heavy AA batteries, and the use of the Auxiliary Territorial Service (ATS) to operate searchlights.

The arrival of women led to complications that now seem strange. Opponents of mixed AA batteries had thought women too frivolous for the idea to succeed, forecasting a disruptive 'musical-comedy-chorus-atmosphere'.

In rationed Britain, the ATS was allocated smaller rations than men, yet the new life made them hungry. "By mutual consent the rations for men and women were pooled and shared equally." On the other hand, huts deemed satisfactory for men were considered too austere for women.

After the Night Blitz, aerial attack lessened. However, while some communities never saw another enemy aircraft for the rest of the war, this was no consolation for those that did. Fierce forays by fighter-bombers against coastal

Airfield names

Zeals, High Post, Acaster Malbis – 60 years ago there were more than 800 aerodromes and landing grounds in the UK. Some were begun before 1939, but most came into being during the war and reverted to farmland or commercial use afterwards. A few huts or an industrial estate with roads like 'Tower View' or 'Spitfire Drive' may now be all there is to show that such a place ever existed. And the name.

Wartime airfields were named after nearby places, and so draw deep from languages spoken across 2,000 years. Trebelsue's syllables are Celtic, Manby's Danish. Wick and Skitten in north-east Scotland have a Norse cadence. Beaulieu evokes Norman-French. Airfield names like Charmy Down, Barton-in-the-Clay, or Stoke Orchard witness contrasting intricacies of Britain's countryside.

Windrush or Appledram can be savoured for their sounds. Marston Moor and Edgehill recollect the Civil War, and an earlier struggle for democracy. Bibury and Northleach are famed for medieval churches. At Moreton Valence is a 12th-century sculpture of St Michael, guardian in the skies. Akeman Street recollects a Roman road. Kelmscott was the home of William Morris. Down Ampney is the name that Vaughan Williams gave to his tune for the hymn *Come Down O Love Divine*.

Since sung at a million weddings, Down Ampney also became the site of an aerodrome whence airborne troops departed for Normandy and Arnhem in 1944.

On one level, such associations are a jumble. On another, they remind us who we are, and why we fought.

Richard Morris

towns, raids from high altitude, the bombing of provincial cities, railway stations and factories all took a toll. In 1942, a year of 'minor' activity, civilian casualties exceeded 7,000.

In early 1944, raids against London resumed. By now, however, defences against conventional attack were supremely efficient. Between June 1944 and March 1945, AA, fighters and balloons together dealt with 4,228 of the estimated 6,725 V1 flying bombs (aka 'doodlebugs') launched against the United Kingdom.

The V2, however, was a different matter. Coded 'Big Ben' by the Allies, the V2 rocket flew at supersonic speed, detonated like a clap of thunder before anyone heard its approach and came like a 'comet from the sky'. Against it, there was no direct defence.

The V2 rocket flew at supersonic speed, detonated like a clap of thunder... and came like a 'comet from the sky'

A last flourish

Sixty years on, the V2 is sometimes remembered as a kind of nasty inconvenience, a sophisticated, yet ultimately futile weapon. Strategically this is true, but it downplays the campaign's scale. During the war's last months there were 1,115 Big Ben incidents in Britain. Most were in London and Essex, but the campaign extended to East Anglia and Kent, while a few penetrated as far inland as Northamptonshire, Bedfordshire and Sussex.

This offensive would have been worse had the Allies not captured northern France in August 1944, so obliging the missiles' launch from further afield and impairing their aim. Even so, they did harm enough. Each was its own tragedy and when the last rocket exploded in Orpington at teatime on March 27 1945, its predecessors had killed 2,854 people.

The V2 is recalled as a last flourish against Britain, yet most of them were aimed at continental targets. The port of Antwerp, in particular, was subjected to furious bombardment – 517 V2s fell on London; Antwerp was hit by more than 1,700.

Britain's blackout was partially relaxed in September 1944. Street lamps glowed for the first time in five years. That they could do so was in part because over a million citizens had been helping each other to hold a roof over Britain. Against conventional attack that roof was now largely secure. Big Ben was the bellwether of the Cold War to come. ■

RH
Thanks

Caring and remembrance

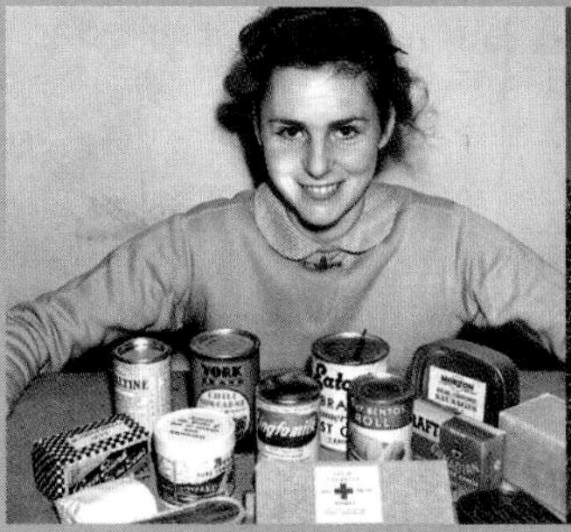
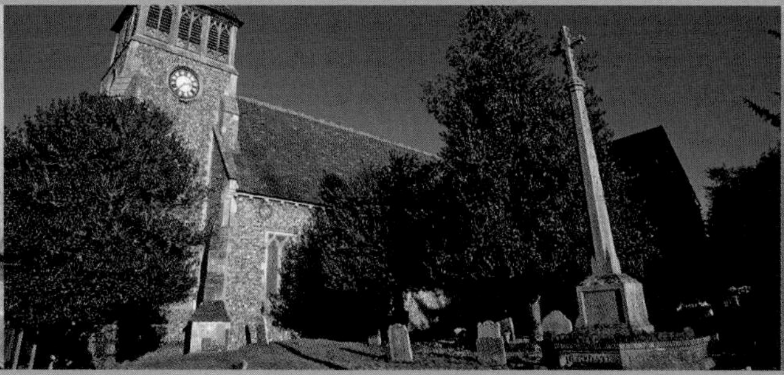
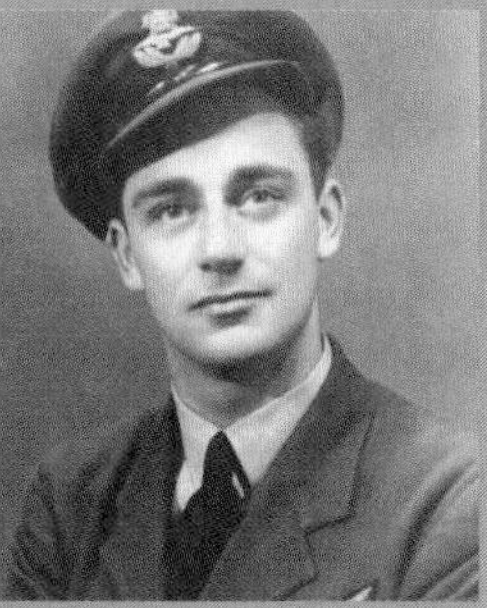

Continuing support

The Royal British Legion provides emotional, financial and social support for those returning from war. Founded in the immediate aftermath of World War I, it continues to help tens of thousands of war veterans who served in World War II. **Andrew Maiden** looks at the direct help given to just a handful of the men and women who secured our freedom in 1945

The Royal British Legion (RBL) is perhaps best known for commemorating the sacrifice that so many made both in the two world wars and in the many conflicts since then, most notably through the annual Remembrance weekend and its associated Poppy Appeal. Inspired by John McCrae's moving poem, *In Flanders' Fields*, the Legion's Poppy Day has been held every November since 1921.

The distribution of over 34 million poppies raises funds for the Legion's work with veterans and their dependents, as well as enabling so many British people to give a personal thank you to those who have served the country.

Help from the Royal British Legion comes in many different forms, from nursing care and counselling, to visits to war graves for veterans and their families. It also extends to benefits advice, job training and loans to set up small businesses, as well as help to get veterans back on their feet financially. In addition, the Legionline helpline ensures that advice is always available at the end of a telephone.

Help from the Royal British Legion comes in many different forms, from nursing care and counselling, to visits to war graves for veterans and their families

After WWII, Trevor Jones left the Welsh Guards to find a severe shortage of housing back home in Wrexham. There were too few homes to go round and the waiting list for council housing stretched for many years, but Trevor was able to benefit from a British Legion housing scheme. A total of 16 homes were built in Borras Park Road and the veterans moving into the houses helped to reduce housing costs by carrying out much of the construction work themselves.

Trevor, who still lives in the street, says: "We had bricklayers, plasterers, joiners and about 40 per cent of the scheme was carried out by us. There were a lot more than 16 people interested but, when it was pointed out that it was going to be built in your spare time, 20 hours a week and would take about three or four years, quite a few fell by the wayside."

Bill Stoneman (left), from Cornwall, served as an RAF gunner from 1942, flying on numerous bombing raids and missions to drop supplies and agents behind enemy lines. He says that there is now a growing awareness of the sacrifices that were made during the war. Invited to speak about his experiences to a group of school children, he said: "I thought if I padded it out, it might go for 20 minutes or so. Over an hour later the kids were still telling me what their grandparents had done in the war." The Legion has helped Bill twice in the past decade. In 1994, he discovered that his deteriorating hearing was caused by tinnitus, which is a common problem for rear gunners. He had not realised that he was entitled to any financial support but the RBL helped him successfully apply for a 20 per cent war pension. More recently, the Legion helped again when his wife was sadly diagnosed with Alzheimer's disease and he took on the role as her principal carer. Bill said: "It certainly takes the stuffing out of you, but they were brilliant and gave me amazing support. I owe them a great debt."

Veterans of WWII that have been helped by the RBL fulfilled many different roles during the conflict. Bombardier Marion McIntosh, for example, worked at the command post at Hellfire Corner in Kent. The post was first in line for enemy bombing raids, which killed many of her friends and colleagues. Today, the women's section of the RBL has helped Marion secure an additional widow's pension, which she describes as a "very nice help".

As well as reacting to veterans' individual needs, the RBL has set up schemes that can help many thousands of people. One such arrangement is the joint venture with The Mobility Bureau to provide electrically powered vehicles (EPVs). The Legion's buying power allows the organisation to offer EPVs at a lower rate, while trained staff can advise users on the most suitable vehicle for them.

George Atkins (above), who served on a Royal Navy U-boat hunter during the war, says: "Without the scooter I'd be confined to the house". During the war, Atkins was posted on HMS *Wild Goose* in the Second Escort Group, seeking out German U-boats in the North Atlantic and protecting the D-Day landing forces. As a result of breathing difficulties, George would have difficulty getting around without his EPV. These stories are replicated countless times across the country, as the RBL provides much-needed support for thousands of unsung British war heroes and heroines. ■

A vital network

The British Red Cross and St. John Ambulance combined to form the Joint War Organisation, playing an essential part in organising supplies and boosting morale. They also helped keep lines of communication open. By **Zac Casey**

The fear and anxiety that must course through the mind of a soldier when captured by the enemy is unimaginable. For a prisoner, merely wanting to let loved ones know that they are alive, or wondering whether anybody will check on their welfare, must surely have been haunting thoughts. How different it is in this modern era of 24-hour communication, where instantaneous information is expected and taken for granted. However, 60 years ago, the flow of information was restricted, particularly if it had the potential to affect wartime morale.

As soon as war broke out, the British Red Cross and St. John Ambulance joined forces to form the Joint War Organisation (JWO), working together as they had done in the South African War and World War I. Their members served as nursing auxiliaries (VADs) at home and abroad, drove ambulances, ran auxiliary hospitals and convalescent homes, delivered emergency aid during the Blitz, gave anti-gas and first aid training and packed prisoner of war (PoW) parcels.

During this time, the JWO acted as a vital conduit between captives and their relatives, a supply line that kept up the morale of hundreds of thousands of British prisoners.

Once a prisoner was registered and contact had been made with their next-of-kin, the JWO, together with the International Committee of the Red Cross (ICRC), were able to keep a channel of communication and supply open between holding camps and the UK. A vital lifeline was established – prisoners were able to receive personal 'next-of-kin' parcels containing soap, clothing and chocolate, which had been packed by family members and then re-packed by JWO volunteers.

Between 1943 and 1945 the JWO distributed over 4,500 tonnes of food aid to the interned. In Britain, this aid supply was co-ordinated by a network of buyers, packers and distributors across the country. Members of an unseen army of volunteers worked constantly – the scale of the situation was immense. Between 1943-44, British prisoners in Europe numbered 180,000. During this period, the JWO made one million food parcels available for British captives.

As the war progressed and the number of prisoners grew, next-of-kin parcels and impromptu deliveries became less reliable, and the now famous Joint War Organisation parcel, also known as the Red Cross parcel, became a regular sight at prison camps. Later, the parcel became more standardised, containing items such as biscuits, tea, jam, sugar and cigarettes – 20 million of these parcels were dispatched in 1945.

Perhaps one of the most important facilities offered by the ICRC is its tracing service. Originally, this service was a

Memories

Alex Lees, 94. Part of the 'Great Escape' team
"The food provided by the Germans was not enough to live on and without the Red Cross parcels, few would have survived. I am more than grateful to the Red Cross for what they did for me and my fellow prisoners."

Jersey began starving between June and December 1944. Relief came in the form of the SS *Vega*, a Swedish ship that sailed to Jersey from Lisbon, bearing Red Cross food parcels for the starving islanders.

Alfred Le Monnier, St. John Ambulance Jersey
"The *Vega* came in towards the end of December 1944. We started unloading it on January 2 1945. St. John Ambulance used to go down to the quay, load up our trolley with these big crates, take them to our stores and unload them, come back and take the trolley again. We did that until the boat was unloaded. They were quite well stacked, the parcels. That's what kept us going. Because I think otherwise we would have died."

British Red Cross volunteer, Parcel Packing Centre in Hove
"The ladies sat at long trestle tables on stools and they packed. Packing meant making sure that the exact number of tins went in. They had to count and put in the exactly stipulated place, each piece of the food parcel. A tin of butter, a tin of preserved meat. There'd be a tin of dried fruit and there'd be chocolate. They were very good parcels."

two-way enquiry and information portal, offering 'mental comfort' to detainees and their families. Naturally, this service was heavily utilised during the course of the war. In 1941, for example, the ICRC's Central Agency for PoWs received and dispatched roughly 10 million communications on behalf of prisoners. This was managed by a staff of 4,300 – 3,500 of which were volunteers. By 1944, in its own words the ICRC was "overwhelmed" by the amount of items it was required to process – the number of sent and received items had doubled to over 20 million.

Each year the ICRC and its regional branches receive tens of thousands of requests for information regarding WWII prisoners held on foreign soil, for example, where relatives were held, where they were laid to rest. This information can often fill wartime gaps that exist in the genealogy of many families. In the UK, the British Red Cross tracing service acts on behalf of UK residents, and the ICRC or respective national societies act on behalf of those residing in other countries, who are trying to find or send a message to family members in the UK. Many searchers have a very vague memory of their missing relative and it is not uncommon for them to have never met. ■

In memoriam

Paul Beaver looks at how the nation remembers the sacrifice of so many

Almost every town and village in this green and pleasant land has its memorial to the fallen. The People's War particularly touched every family and community. True, World War I (WWI) has its masonry that remembers the dead of that first 20th-century conflict, but it was still a conflict of the battlefield. World War II (WWII) was truly a world war that encompassed town and village, field and beach, factory worker and farmer, and, of course, all the services.

Take a tour around today's United Kingdom and find the memorials. They come in many shapes and sizes, from stained-glass windows in churches to village crosses, dedicated to the fallen.

Some remember key events, like the Battle of Britain, which raged over the skies of Britain, particularly the Home Counties, from July 10 until October 31 1940. It is remembered in the windows of the parish church at Biggin Hill (Kent) or in the porch of the Officers' Mess at RAF Bentley Priory (Middlesex), the headquarters of RAF Fighter Command for the duration.

The armed services have devoted much time and effort to keeping alive the memories of those gallant men and women that sacrificed their lives for freedom's cause. In November every year, it is not just the Cenotaph in Whitehall that sees ceremonies of remembrance, but churches and chapels across the land.

The military garrison churches are especially blessed with fine memorials and veterans still return to remember their comrades. Those left behind also find comfort in the simple inscriptions, the glass windows, the painted boards and the flags.

Lest we forget

It is not just the home front that is remembered with such loving dignity. Across the country, across the Commonwealth, there are the memorials to the thousands of servicemen and women who perished in far-flung battlefields. From the steaming jungles of Burma to the Arctic wastes of the Northern Norwegian Sea, we remember those who gave their lives for freedom. There are graveyards and other memorials in Palestine, Cyprus, Burma, India, Afghanistan and the Falkland Islands.

Many people still travel every year to the memorials in France: from WWI in Flanders; the Normandy beaches and the campaigns for the liberation of that country during WWII. There are memorials and graveyards, many cared for by foreign nationals and supervised by the War Graves Commissioners, in far-flung corners.

On a winding road from Bucharest to Brasov, in Romania, there is a small cemetery for the crews of two Liberator bombers of the Royal Air Force, shot down while raiding nearby oil refineries that produced fuel for the Nazi war machine. These graves were tended throughout the Iron Curtain period after WWII; the Union Flag raised and lowered every day by locals keen to remember those who helped liberate their nation. Passing military staff cars even stop and officers walk to the graves and salute.

Travelling along a road, almost a track, cut into the fine limestone rock of Cyprus, it is hard to see the

Civilians Remembered Trust

The Civilians Remembered Trust is constructing the first memorial dedicated to some 60,000 British civilians lost to World War II – many remain uncounted. Sixty thousand fibre-optic lights will create the 'Path of Stars' and a glass pavilion will house an educational exhibition highlighting the roles of the civilians during the war. Designed by Piers Gough, the park in Hermitage Wharf in Wapping was originally a bomb shelter and a perfect place for the memorial.

Lauren Rose-Smith

Across the country there are memorials to the thousands of servicemen and women who perished in battle

memorials made from that same rock in a small grove of olive trees. Finding the gate and entering is to learn a lesson about those forgotten parts of the world that suffered war but did not hit the headlines, like Burma, Dunkirk or Normandy did.

Visit the small Dutch town of Arnhem in September and witness the most incredible sight of local school children attending to the graves of the fallen of the Parachute and Air Landing Divisions, which so nearly forced the pace of the war in Europe in 1944. Famous for the 'Bridge Too Far', the town and its outlying villages support memorials, museums and the graves of units long since gone from the British order of Battle, such as the Glider Pilot Regiment and the Oxfordshire & Buckingham Regiment (the Ox and Bucks).

Across the Thames near Windsor, on the flightpath out of London Heathrow, is the Runnymede Memorial to the many thousands of Royal Air Force aircrew, especially members of Bomber and Coastal Commands who have no known final resting place. It is set on a hill overlooking the Thames and meadows on which an earlier generation had stood up for Freedom's Cause, 800 years before. The Royal Navy and Merchant Navy also have their memorials to those who have no grave but who perished at sea.

This September, the Thames will see another memorial to join those to the Fleet Air Arm, the Chindits, the Royal Tank Regiment and the Royal Air Force, when the Battle of Britain Memorial is unveiled. The nation remembers with pride and sorrow those who died to give us a future. ■

Acknowledgements

Air Vice Marshal David Pocock Defence Services Secretary and Commemoration Events Director, Ministry of Defence, wishes to thank the following:

Project team

Commodore Geoff Edwardes OBE RN	Deputy Commemoration Events Director
Wing Commander Chris Pickthall RAF	Assistant Commemoration Events Director
Mr Gareth Legg	Budgets, Resources and Event Attendance
Major Andrew Poë RGJ	St James's Park
Mr Mike Delaney	Veterans Awareness Week
David Collins	Database Manager
Lieutenant Colonel Andrew Ford WG	Westminster Abbey Producer
Lieutenant Colonel Geoff Kingston	Director of Music and Bands
Major Peter Hunter LG	Protocol and Transport
Major Matthew Middleditch QGM RLC	Technical Site Manager
Squadron Leader Michael Buckland RAF	Flypasts Manager
Squadron Leader Karen Prichard RAF	Security
Squadron Leader Dave Scorer RAF	Programmes
Lieutenant John Hesketh RN	Navy Protocol
Captain Simon Holden RA	Army Protocol
Flight Lieutenant Jaswant Bhangu RAF	Staff Officer
Flight Lieutenant Ellis Williams RAF	RAF Protocol
Flight Lieutenant Gerry Cepelak RAF	Accommodation
Flight Lieutenant Bruce Thompson RAF	Standards and Banners
Flying Officer Anna Layton RAF	Service Support
Warrant Officer 1 Tony Fernandez RN	Veterans Awareness Week
Charlotte Henwood	Curator of Exhibition of WW2 Art
Sergeant John West	Office Manager

Ministry of Defence Media, DGMC

Air Commodore Mike Lloyd RAF	Director of Defence Publicity
Colonel Paul Brook	Media Operation
Group Captain David Prowse RAF	Deputy Director Defence Publicity
Mrs Melissa Maynard	Public Relations Manager
Mr Howard Rhoades	
Mr Ray Manning Lewis	
Ms Carol Rockey	
Mr Chris Roberts	
Squadron Leader Steve Rovery RAF	
Mr Greg Spring	

Veterans Mrs Carolyn Short and the Veterans' Services Team at the Veterans' Agency ticketing and co-ordinating National Events

Lieutenant Colonel Chris Davis RM	Principal Director of Music Headquarters Band Services Royal Marines
Major Philip Watson RM	Director of Music Band of Her Majesty's Royal Marines Portsmouth (Royal Band)
Captain Peter Curtis RM	Director of Music Band of Her Majesty's Royal Marines Commando Training Centre Royal Marines
Major Robert Owen	Director of Music Band of the Welsh Guards
Major Douglas Robertson	Director of Music Band of the Blues and Royals
Major Tim Arnold	Director of Music Minden Band of the Queen's Division
Wing Commander Steward Stirling RAF	Principal Director of Music Headquarters Royal Air Force Music Services

Unusual Services Ltd

Executive Producer	Alan Jacobi LVO
Project Manager	Malcolm Birkett
Project Administrator	David Mayo
Production Accountant	Brian Rose
Production Manager	Simon Burnett
Site Manager	Lindsay Barrowclough
Production Assistant	Sherri Gordon
Health & Safety	Caroline Barrowclough
Commemoration Show Producer	Simon Brooks-Ward LVO OBE TD
Commemoration Show Director	Dougie Squires
Show Administrator	Isobel Hatton
Sound Design	John Del'Nero
Lighting Design	Alan Thomson
Stage Management	Simon Garrett
Living Museum Producer	Sheelagh Barnard
Living Museum Production Manager	Ted Irwin
Vehicle Display Co-ordinator	George Douglas MBE
Veterans Centre Production Manager	Mark Houghton
Projection Show Producer	Sheelagh Barnard
Projection Realisation	Ross Ashton

Special thanks to all the contractors who have played an essential role in bringing this event to fruition; and to WCC Special Events, Metropolitan Police, Royal Parks, London Ambulance, St John Ambulance, Red Cross, Salvation Army, London Underground, London Buses, Transport for London.

Many people and organisations have been involved in this WWII Event, if you have not been credited please accept our apologies – we are nonetheless grateful for all the support, assistance and enthusiasm that you have all given to the project.

The MoD Commemorations Team also wishes to thank:

gettyimages

LAND-ROVER

Supported by

War is over!

The end of the war brought massive celebrations nationwide as everyone breathed a collective sigh of relief. Parties erupted on every street corner, pubs ran dry and huge crowds gathered in the cities to rejoice that the war was finally over. By Louise Drew

On May 8 1945 Winston Churchill made a radio broadcast announcing that war in Europe was finally at an end.

Floods of people converged on some of London's great monuments, floodlit specially for the occasion. There were fireworks, and effigies of Hitler burned on bonfires around the capital.

Huge crowds, many dressed in red, white and blue, gathered outside Buckingham Palace in London and cheered as the King, Queen and their family came out onto the balcony.

Across the country, blackout curtains were ripped from windows, lights were finally turned on and families, friends, neighbours and complete strangers shared their joy at hearing the news that it was over.

In the suburbs, children's parties were thrown, with furniture and tables brought into the street, and races and other events organised for after tea.

Crowds gathered in public places to sing and dance, and alcohol flowed freely as everyone tried to shake off their recent past and look forward to a brighter, more peaceful future.

But it was not until August 15, when Japan surrendered to the Allies, that the world could join in with the celebrations. The day was officially declared Victory in Japan day. World War II had come to an end.

With the announcement of the end of the war the nation was united once more – in relief, in joy, in sadness, in pride and in celebration. ■

Publisher's thanks

Newsdesk Communications and the Ministry of Defence gratefully acknowledge the invaluable support of the following companies, without whom this commemorative publication would not have been possible.

Anglo Irish Bank	108
BAE Systems	8
Bibby Line	28
Bletchley Park Trust	142
Boeing	24
Bristow Helicopters	84
Britam Defence	49
British Airways	4
BT	73
Bucharest Stock Exchange	174
Capgemini	46
Chevrolet	69
Christy Group	180
Cobra	130
Compass/ESS	33
DICoD/Ministry for War Veterans	56
Duxford Flying Legends	193
EWS	140
Filtronic	145
Bottle Green	119
GCHQ	140
GNER	148
HBOS	6
Imperial War Museum	164
InterContinental Hotels	16
Jacobs	10
JCB	151
Kier	79
London Fire Brigade	76
Maersk	2
Malta Tourism	120
Manchester City Council	129
Marks & Spencer	22
Marshall Aerospace	63
Marylebone Cricket Club (MCC)	116
McDonald's	83
Ministry of Defence	103
News International Newspapers Ltd.	39
Parker Hannifin	12
Parker Pens	21
PDSA	168
Plymouth Gin	133
Polish Embassy	154
Prague Stock Exchange	134
QinetiQ	14
Reliance Precision	152
Ribena	113
Ricardo	157
Rubens Hotel	177
Selenia Communications	171
Severn Trent	26
Singapore Tourism Board	163
Sodexho	184
SSAFA	28
SSVC	199
The British Army	97
The Kennel Club	114
The Royal Air Force	100
The Royal Navy	90
The Sloane Club	138
The Thistle Foundation	183
TNT Express	124
Transport for London	162
UEFA	200
VT Group	44
Zurich Municipal	64